n or rene   b

UNIONS AND UNIVERSITIES

UNIONS
AND
UNIVERSITIES

THE RISE OF THE
NEW LABOR LEADER

Joel Denker

ALLANHELD, OSMUN MONTCLAIR

ALLANHELD, OSMUN & CO. PUBLISHERS, INC.

Published in the United States of America in 1981
by Allanheld, Osmun & Co. Publishers, Inc.
6 South Fullerton Avenue, Montclair, New Jersey 07042
A Division of Littlefield, Adams & Company

Copyright © 1981 by Joel Denker

Library of Congress Cataloging in Publication Data

Denker, Joel.
   Unions and universities.

   Revision of thesis (doctoral)—Harvard University,
1978.
   Bibliography: p.
   Includes index.
   1. Industrial relations—Study and teaching (Higher)—
United States.   I. Title.
HD6960.5.U5D45   1981   331'.07'1173   80-67093
ISBN 0-916672-58-1   AACR2

Printed in the United States of America

*To the memory of William Abbott,
an exemplary human being and labor educator*

Contents

Foreword

Over most of the century and a half since the courts stopped classifying unions as illegal conspiracies, labor and higher education have had a tenuous relationship, characterized on both sides by distrust and usually also by disdain.

That is hardly surprising since the trade union movement, until just a few years ago, regarded the workplace and the picket line as the only worthwhile training grounds for union leadership. The universities and colleges, in labor's view, were elitist institutions coddled by the business and financial establishment for the primary, if not exclusive, purpose of enshrining values that would perpetuate its domination over the economy.

University administrators and trustees, for their part, took an equally negative view of the labor movement. Unions by definition were fomenters of discontent, run by leaders whose proud boast was their lack of book learning—men obviously ill equipped to make any useful contribution to the planning of college curricula or to the objective inculcation of knowledge.

The relationship is not nearly so antagonistic now. Part of the explanation lies in the extent to which the rapid growth in the size, number, and scope of state universities, colleges, and community colleges and the simultaneous mushrooming of scholarship and research funds from the public treasury have made both mainstays of the whole structure of higher education, with labor as a principal lobbyist for this expansion in government's role. Another part lies in the increased complexity of the union leader's own function and in the function of the organization he heads. Unionists have been obliged to recognize, however reluctantly, that the dimensions of their involvement in law, money management, contract enforcement, problems of international trade, and a host of other inescapable interactions with politics and the community require a range of expertise much broader than can be picked up on the job in factory or office.

These changes have brought a measure of rapport, but the relationship between labor and academe remains prickly— the mutual discomfort heightened by the confusion of goals that still bedevils labor education in all its phases. Should it be primarily a counterpart—oriented toward the training of a trade union elite—of the schools of business that are becoming a must as upward way stations for budding corporate executives who will be skilled in marshalling money, markets, and manpower into patterns that will advance the profitability and growth of their enterprises?

Or should the core of labor education be a concentration on the rank and file, with courses aimed at helping union members to better themselves in their jobs in industry or government and thus climb the employment ladder faster toward supervisory or administrative responsibilities? Or should it be an instrument for giving a new generation of unionists, many of them delivered over by their employers under contracts that make union membership mandatory as a condition of holding their jobs, an awareness of the struggles that went into winning those contracts and lifting the standards they guarantee?

Or, yet again, should labor studies at the university level provide a forum and a research setting for reappraising the policies and directions of both organized labor and the larger society? The adversarial tradition that has made unions think of themselves as permanently at war with management was always a deterrent to internal debate on where unionism was going and where it was going wrong, but the multiplicity of new problems created by the changing nature of work and of America's relative position in an increasingly competitive and unsettled world makes the need for reassessment within labor omnipresent.

In this fascinating and timely book, Joel Denker, who has managed to crowd a lot of personal experience in labor education into a decade or so of adulthood, provides worthwhile perspectives on the dilemmas presented for both unions and universities by the still ill-focused efforts to build bridges linking these two fundamental props of our society in ways that will provide more expert and responsible leaders from the trade union movement.

He explores such idealistic early experiments as the Brookwood Labor College, which saw social reform as a key element of its mission but which finally succumbed to the hostile conviction of the old American Federation of Labor hierarchy of the 1920s and 1930s that the college represented a threat to the sovereign right of unions to establish their own policies and principles unimpeded by intellectual second-guessers. No similar threat was seen in the Wisconsin School for Workers, which reflected the "utilitarian idealism" of John R. Commons and his protégé at the University of Wisconsin, Selig Perlman.

That school steered away from ideology and thus avoided conflict with a pragmatic movement dedicated to bread-and-butter unionism but, happily, given an extra dose of yeast in Wisconsin by the populism of that state's farmer-labor tradition. The legal foundation put under collective bargaining by the New Deal, the unionization of the mass production industries, the introduction by the War Labor Board of employer-financed welfare programs, the postwar spread of social security under the union label, all multiplied the union need not only for lawyers and other technicians but for more professionalism in union executive suites.

The difficulties of adjustment posed for unions by these developments are sympathetically analyzed in these pages. The difficulties were equally great for academics. The rigidities of recognized scholastic disciplines were defended by purists within university faculties as zealously as if they were journeymen in the building trades resisting a scaling down of apprenticeship standards to ease entry for outsiders. A raft of new problems has been introduced into the development of labor studies programs by the swift expansion in civil service unionism, with membership priorities that often differ greatly from those of unions in the private sector. These problems, too, are analyzed with the useful insights the author has derived from intimate experience at a university in the heart of the nation's capital, the center of both the Federal establishment and the labor movement.

Nothing more eloquently attests the importance of the subject than the fact that this volume appears just when labor is itself turning more and more toward leadership by men and women whose credentials include college degrees as well as callouses acquired at the work bench. It should provide priceless perspective for every reader concerned with intelligent resolution of the problems that still obstruct a fruitful union of labor education and higher education.

A. H. Raskin

Preface

The signs of acceptance of university training in the labor movement are omnipresent. More union presidents now than in the past have gone to college or hold a degree. J. C. Turner, president of the International Union of Operating Engineers, got his union card while working his way through Catholic University in Washington, D.C. Both Lane Kirkland and Thomas Donahue, president and secretary-treasurer, respectively, of the AFL-CIO, are college graduates. (Mr. Donahue also has a law degree.) George Meany, past president of the AFL-CIO, never graduated from high school. Increasingly, unions are going outside their ranks to hire academically trained staff not only for specialized positions but also for the politically important posts of business agent and organizer. These developments represent a departure from the union tradition that experience, not formal training, is the best preparation for labor leadership.

Not to be outdistanced by their own rank and file, a membership that is better educated than ever before, union officials are seeking further education for themselves. Graduates of labor studies programs in community colleges in San

Francisco and Baltimore have emphasized their degrees in their campaigns for union office. In the volatile politics of local unions, where elections are often hotly contested, a credential, once a detriment, may give one candidate the edge.

Labor studies programs are burgeoning in colleges and universities. The most recent count showed that 47 institutions either awarded a degree—an A.A., B.A., or M.A.—or offered a major in the field.[1] In 1964 no degree programs existed. Present and prospective union officials seeking degrees are taking classes in such areas as labor history, labor and politics, collective bargaining, and labor law. Traditionally, university labor programs had been exclusively preoccupied with providing short, noncredit courses in the techniques of union leadership.

The skills required by the trade union leader, advocates of credit in labor studies argue, are as worthy of certification as those employed by management. The UAW Education Department puts the value of the associate degree in labor studies, the degree it is promoting in community colleges, in just these terms:

> It is not the degree itself, but what the degree means. The professional qualifications of the labor leaders merit the same respect by colleges and the public as those of other occupations. Besides, the degree means that the holder is judged to be qualified in his field. For the Associate Degree in Labor Studies, it will mean that a usable understanding of the social, political and economic environment of his work has been reached, and that these are the basis of improved ability as a union leader and negotiator.[2]

This book will examine these phenomena from a number of vantage points, perspectives that do justice to the partners in this most unlikely marriage, the union and the university. It will underline the dilemmas inherent in the quest of a new field, labor studies, for acceptance in the academy. Most important, it will investigate what the rise of academic training reveals about the changing character of the American union.

I have used unconventional sources, materials that illustrate both the infancy and the amorphousness of the field. I have drawn on my interviews with labor educators, notes on meetings and conferences, reports and evaluations of university programs, newsletters, and speeches given at labor education gatherings.

I have more than an academic interest in the subject. Wherever possible, I weave my own experiences of labor education into my analysis. The case study I use to illustrate the issues involved in creating an academic discipline—my account of the development of a master's degree in labor studies at the University of the District of Columbia—is one in which I actively participated. I was appointed Associate Professor of Labor Studies at Federal City College (now the University of the District of Columbia) in September 1975. I am now beginning my sixth year in that post. In that position, I have had a major responsibility in the shaping of a proposal for a master's degree and in the campaign to win its adoption. Now funded, the program will begin its first class in January 1981.

I got my exposure to labor education in the course of two other jobs. I taught labor history in the evening undergraduate program of the Rutgers University Labor Education Center, an established institute with strong ties to New Jersey's labor movement. I also worked for the American Studies Department at the State University of New York, College at Old Westbury, organizing a labor studies component for their program. The Westbury program was striking for its academic leadership, and for its lack of roots in the labor community.

Meeting and talking with many of the leading practitioners, watching the field define itself at many meetings and conferences, I have gained a valuable perspective from which to observe the birth pangs of labor studies. First-hand experience has provided a touchstone against which to test my developing theories and assumptions about labor education and its relationship to the union movement.

Notes

1. Lois Gray, "Academic Degrees for Labor Studies: A New Goal for Unions," *Monthly Labor Review* 100, no. 6 (June 1977): 16.
2. *Workers "Opportunity" college*, UAW Education Department, n.d., p. 10.

Acknowledgments

I began this study as my final doctoral paper for the Harvard University Graduate School of Education. It was submitted in 1978. This book results from a thorough revision and expansion of that work. Substantial new material has been added. I appreciate the comments and support offered by the three members of my doctoral committee: my adviser, David Cohen, Nathan Glazer, and Stephan Thernstrom.

I am indebted to veteran labor educators Larry Rogin, Russell Allen, William Abbott, and Herbert Levine for the insights I have gained from discussions with them. The late William Abbott, to whom this volume is dedicated, was always sympathetic to a younger person in the field and imparted much of the lore he acquired during his career. John MacKenzie, the director of the Labor Studies Center at the University of the District of Columbia, has been generous in sharing with me his observations on labor education and experiences in the field. My work at the Labor Studies Center has been an ideal apprenticeship and one that made this study possible.

When I decided to turn my doctoral work into a book,

xviii   **Acknowledgments**

David Brody, Nathan Glazer, William Kornblum, and David
Riesman offered strong encouragement. Harvey Friedman
and Lois Gray provided valuable assistance. I have learned a
great deal from my students in both my graduate labor studies
courses and my labor extension classes.

I am grateful to Judith DeSerio for enabling me to use the
library at the American Council on Educiation, where I did
much of the writing and research for this book. Deanthia
Mebane and Mathew Simon performed heriocally on typing
the manuscript.

UNIONS AND UNIVERSITIES

1

University Labor Education: The Historical Tradition

The defining quality of labor education today is that it is institutional training conducted largely by trade unions or university labor programs individually or in concert to meet the organizational requirements of unions. They run short, functional programs—weekend conferences, six-week classes, one-week summer schools—for an audience of union officials and activists. The training includes grievance handling, union administration, bargaining, and parliamentary procedure. In addition to stressing skills, it tries to cement the loyalty of members to their organizations.

University labor extension stands out in sharp relief when compared to representative programs in the "workers' education" movement of the 1920s.[1] Independent residential schools, socialist and industrial trade unions, women imbued with the settlement-house ethic, progressive social scientists, adult educators—all contributed to the rambuctiousness of the movement. Many of its guiding spirits in the open-shop era were rebels who were critical of the complacency of the AFL. The irreverent tone of much of workers' education contrasts

1

with the more cautious efforts of university labor education centers to follow the established policies of organized labor.

The curriculum of workers' education, rooted in the social sciences and humanities, was offered through the format of long-term residential schools. The leaders of the movement saw education as a way to inspire social awareness; thus it provided more than a set of useful techniques. Many of the prominent programs defined their constituency to include the unorganized workers in industry, whom the dominant craft unions disdained.

The Brookwood Experiment

> If you are discouraged about labor's future, if you have lost hope, pay a visit to Brookwood Labor College. . . . You will be surprised. You will be thrilled. . . . It's a big place, a live place. It's not "red." It's not reactionary. It teaches facts—not theories; conditions—not propaganda. . . . Yes it's quite refreshing.
> —The Editor, *Journal of Electrical Workers and Operators*, March 1926

Brookwood Labor College and the Wisconsin School for Workers in Industry typified two important strands of the workers' education movement. Brookwood represented its gadfly role, its abrasive challenge to the labor orthodoxy of the day. The Wisconsin project was an example of the effort by good-spirited friends of labor to offer a general education to unorganized workers. It evolved into the School for Workers, the longest continuous university labor-education program, whose orientation was vastly different both from its predecessor and from Brookwood. (The University of California at Berkeley started the first labor extension service in 1920, which lapsed and was reestablished after World War II.)

Both projects had one important quality in common: They were launched without the backing of the mainstream of the labor movement, and each received major funding from outside organized labor. Although countless labor colleges sprouted in cities during the 1920s, promoted by local and state central labor councils, Brookwood Labor College, established in 1921, was the first permanent residential school. It offered a two-year program rather than the format of evening classes provided by the city colleges. The city labor colleges often used the services of faculty from nearby colleges, such as Amherst, Harvard, and MIT. Brookwood, however, had a full-time staff.

Brookwood represented that unique alliance of progressive trade unionists and sympathetic intellectuals that distinguished workers' education during this period. Unlike the labor education programs of today, Brookwood and similar ventures operated in constant opposition to the stands of the American Federation of Labor. Although much of its financial support came from the liberal Garland Fund, it received funds and endorsements from individual unions, such as the Railway Clerks, the Machinists, the AFT (American Federation of Teachers), the ILGWU (International Ladies Garment Workers Union), the Painters, and the Brewery Workers, as well as from a number of state and city bodies. Brookwood drew the largest number of students from expanding industrial unions in the needle trades and mining. Clergyman and activist A. J. Muste chaired the faculty, all of whom were members of Local 189, the workers'-education local of the AFT. Teachers included David Saposs, a student of University of Wisconsin economist John R. Commons, Tom Tippett, a former education director of the UMW (United Mine Workers), and Mark Starr, who had worked with the National Council of Labor Colleges in England. The influence of visiting scholars like Horace Kallen, Sumner Slichter, and Reinhold Niebuhr rubbed off on the school.[2]

Brookwood's educational program combined a strong practical orientation with the skeptical flavor of the new social science. The school trained its students in the organizing and administrative skills required in union building, such as "how to keep minutes and write resolutions; how to conduct a meeting, how to organize a strike, provide relief, secure fair publicity for the cause."[3] Some, like Victor Reuther, went on to become leaders in the CIO. Brookwood offered courses in labor journalism and organizing along with the social sciences, such as sociology and economics, the standard fare of the workers' education programs of the 1920s.

Although the majority of students at Brookwood were union members, the school saw its mission as preparing students to enlist unorganized workers in the union cause. Conferences sponsored by the school focused on the low-level of organization among youth and women workers. Some Brookwood spokesmen like James Maurer, a plumber who was president of the Pennsylvania Federation of Labor and candidate for vice-president of the Socialist Party, saw workers' education as an integral part of an even broader social commitment:

> Labor education aims at the ultimate liberation of the working masses. . . . Unless it is education which looks toward a new order of society, with more wisdom and justice than is found in our present order, its right to existence is questionable.[4]

This view was shared by the International Ladies Garment Workers and the Amalgamated Clothing Workers, the unions most identified with the movement. They were the first unions to establish education departments—the ILGWU in 1916, the Amalgamated in 1919.[5] The leaders of these departments infused them with a socialist vision. Fannia Cohn, secretary of the ILGWU education department, portrayed workers' education as "a movement for special education . . . which will enable the workers to accomplish their special job which is to change economic and social conditions so that those who produce shall own the product of their labor."[6] Simultaneously, the school clung to both an activist philosophy and to a pedagogy that was skeptical of all orthodoxies. Brookwood's bylaws stated that

Teachers are to be accorded the fullest possible freedom to investigate and set forth the truth, since it is clearly understandable that a school carried on under the auspices of the labor movement and serving that movement should fall into the same error of suppressing freedom of thought and expression which the labor movement and intelligent educationalists deplore in the case of other institutions of learning.[7]

Inevitably, Brookwood's ambition to increase the number of organized workers and to leave no ideologies or points of view unexamined collided with the AFL's own interests as protector of craft unionism. Brookwood's assumptions clashed with the AFL's determination to set the boundaries for acceptable debate in the labor movement. The permanent Committee on Education of the AFL stated in 1928:

In the development of worker's education a number of facts have become clear. The first of these is the importance of restricting interference with the trade union's final and absolute right to determine its own policy. The principle is inherent in the philosophy of the American trade union movement; it is the basis of its insistence on voluntarism and local autonomy.[8]

Antagonism between the two parties continued to build and culminated in the decision of the AFL Executive Council on October 29, 1928, to advise its affiliates to sever their ties with Brookwood. Although Brookwood continued until 1937, it did so without the blessings of the AFL. Despite the pressure, many of the unions that had supported Brookwood remained loyal.

The AFL also moved to stamp out independent tendencies in the Workers Education Bureau, the organization founded in 1921 as the coordinating arm for the budding workers' education movement. Originally under the sway of workers' education programs and state and local central bodies, exponents of industrial unionism and training for "social thinking," the WEB had become the educational arm of the AFL by

1929. In that year the AFL and its associated national unions maneuvered to get enough votes between them to win effective control of the organization.[9]

Now the AFL had enough leverage to censor any publication that did not square with the policy it had imposed on the WEB. In its new role as a "neutral" educational and research organization, the Executive Council of the WEB expelled Brookwood from the body in 1929. At the direction of the AFL Executive Council, the WEB convention in April 1929 supported extension divsons of state universities rather than labor colleges as the preferred location for workers' education.[10]

The distance between the movement and the official labor leadership is underscored in AFL President William Green's derisive comments on a "Workers' Education Convention":

> a Workers' Education Convention cannot be measured by the same standard as that found in a Trade Union convention or in a convention of the American Federation of Labor. An "Education" convention is made up of different types of people than those who attend a Trade Union Convention. Many of those who attend an Education convention look at matters from a theoretical and academic point of view while those who attend Trade Union Conventions are practical men and women dealing with Trade Union problems in a practical way. We cannot help but draw the line of distinction between those who are drawn to an educational conference and those who represent trade unions in a trade union convention.[11]

The School for Workers:
The Origins of University Labor Extension

If Brookwood represented the dedication of the workers' education movement to organization-building skills, the Wisconsin School for Workers in Industry embodied the spirit of educational uplift associated with the "gentle ladies," the educators of upper-middle-class background who pioneered the women's programs of that era. The Wisconsin project, which instituted a six-week resident summer school for working girls in 1925, was informed by the same kind of humanistic mission as the Bryn Mawr Summer School, started in 1921:

> The aim of the school is to offer young women in industry opportunities to study liberal subjects and to train themselves in clear thinking; to stimulate an active and continued interest in problems of our economic order; to develop a desire for study as a means of understanding and of enjoyment of life.[12]

Bryn Mawr's goal was to attract a student body evenly divided between organized and unorganized workers.[13]

Recruited through the Industrial Girls Clubs of the YWCA, primarily nonunion working women studied a curriculum that contained heavy doses of literature, drama, and composition, as well as social science. Scholarships and funds for the program were raised by the YWCA, whose Industrial Division recruited most of the women students for the early residential schools. (The Industrial Division was also an important source of teachers in the workers' education programs.[14]) Women's organizations like the YWCA did much to determine the direction of the movement. The Women's Trade Union League, started in 1903 by affluent Eastern women in the tradition of noblesse oblige, established what some consider to be the first classes for unionized workers.[15]

The school's emphasis began to shift in 1928, when, under its new name, School for Workers, it filled the vacuum left by the collapse of the 11 labor colleges started in Wisconsin during the 1920s. The State Federation of Labor, upset about the small number of organized workers in the school, asked Professor John R. Commons, chairman of the faculty committee of the School for Women Workers, to persuade the university to offer its services to the unionized workers. The school became co-ed, and by 1933 men were a majority.

Unionized workers replaced the unorganized as the school's constituency.[16]

Increasingly, union leadership sought out the programs; in 1941 union officers comprised 86.5 percent of the students. No longer dependent on the goodwill of outside philanthropy, the school tapped union treasuries to provide student scholarships. Between 1928 and 1932 union financial support had grown from almost nothing to 100 percent of student assistance.[17]

The curriculum and format naturally changed dramatically. Economics, confidence-building courses in public speaking and parliamentary procedure, and training in grievance handling and union administration supplanted the old liberal arts offerings. A series of two-week noncredit institutes jointly planned and tailored to the needs of specific unions gradually replaced the interunion six-week summer session. Other independent schools that survived during the 1930s made similar alterations to respond to the organizational demands of unions capitalizing on the favorable climate fostered by the Wagner Act and the New Deal. The Hudson Shore Labor School, which inherited Bryn Mawr's program in 1939, shortened the summer school and placed emphasis on the practical training desired by individual unions.[18]

The unions' priority of establishing their institutional strength, including training new leadership and recruiting new members, changed their conception of education. The ILGWU, the adherent of general education, began an initiation program in 1937 and required it of new members and officers. Training in steward's skills, public speaking, or parliamentary procedure seemed self-evidently practical when compared with the more elusive benefits of the humanities.

The Wisconsin program that emerged in the 1930s had more in common with the hard-headed outlook of the trade union colleges than it did with the YWCA ethic. The objective of the workers' college in Milwaukee was:

to train economists, statisticians, organizers and speakers from our own ranks, with our own point of view, who are fully capable of representing our interests.[19]

Ernest Schwartztrauber, the first director of the school, captured the difference in style when he quoted representative statements from students in 1925 and 1935 who were applying for scholarships:

1925

to better myself for my work

to give me a wide outlook on life

to regain the power of concentration, and to become more self-confident

1935

to learn more about the workings of unionism

I feel that a school of this kind would prepare me to work better in my union and among other youth

because if possible I wish to make a career in the labor field.[20]

Wisconsin's brand of social science, its institutional emphasis and public policy orientation, and the university's land-grant philosophy left their imprint on the School for Workers. The impulse that led John R. Commons (who along with Selig Perlman had an immense influence on the development of the school) to advise the socialist administration in Milwaukee, to draft the state's first industrial safety and workmens' compensation law, and to serve on the commission set up to enforce it, is also illuminated in his support of the School for Workers. Schwartztrauber called him a man of "utilitarian idealism."[21]

The knowledge that the university furnished to commissions and boards in its role as an "asset of the state," to use Wisconsin's president C. R. Van Hise's phrase, should just as appropriately go to unions, another indispensable part of the institutional fabric. Commons believed that the knowledge born of social-science research could serve institutions in carrying on their policy making and administrative functions. How apt it was for an economist, whose study of labor history made its centerpiece the union as an institution, to be associated with the first substantial effort of an American university to provide services to organized workers.

Wisconsin's trade unions felt that it was inconsistent for the university to run programs for farmers and deny them to urban workers. Wisconsin had established an experiment station in 1883, and it was a pioneer in agricultural extension. The state's dairy industry, for example, received a boost from the university in its drive for modernization. The university's role as an evenhanded dispenser of expertise to interest groups, as "a kind of 'consulting engineer' in the public life of the state of Wisconsin," to quote one journal, made partnership with the unions logical.[22]

The Wisconsin experience was unique. The university had assets that few others possessed. In addition to a progressive tradition, it had an institutionally oriented economics department, an agricultural extension service, and the influence of socialist trade unions. The match between the School for Workers' functional style, its eschewing of ideology, and the bread-and-butter demands of Wisconsin's trade unions made for the harmony with the mainstream of the labor movement that Brookwood never achieved. The school fashioned a model of labor education, one that was determinedly pragmatic in its emphasis on nuts-and-bolts training, which university programs developed in quite different settings after World War II would refine and expand.

The Postwar Era:
The Rise of Industrial Relations

Labor extension centers, which blossomed on state university campuses in the postwar period, frequently were housed in the inhospitable setting of institutes of industrial relations. Extension programs were at a disadvantage in the contest for university resources, with industrial relations institutes riding the crest of the wave of the movement for "labor peace." Casting themselves as impartial arbiters in the labor-management conflict, the proponents of industrial relations were more popular with university administrators than were the advocates of interest-group training. The ideological debate between these rivals was part of a larger battle for power and recognition. A loss for labor education, its supporters feared, would mean stepchild status for university services to trade unions.[23]

Industrial relations had first gained a foothold on the campus as part of a foundation-sponsored effort to modernize the personnel function of large corporations. The Rockefeller and Earhart foundations funded industrial relations divisions at Yale, Princeton, Stanford, and other universities between 1922 and 1938. These research institutes were designed to bolster the work of the new personnel and industrial relations departments that had been established by companies during World War I and in the 1920s.[24]

The sophisticated corporate leadership of firms like International Harvester, Standard Oil, and Bethlehem Steel recognized that systematic attention paid to the needs of workers would reap dividends in greater productivity and profits. Successful management, as Charles Schwab, the chief of Bethlehem, put it, "is going to depend more and more upon the management of men than upon the organization of machines and other problems of practical engineering."[25] Corporations downgraded the responsibilities of first-line supervisors, many of whom had risen from the ranks, and centralized the tasks of testing, hiring, training, and promotion in departments run by experts. Industrial relations departments also were given the job of running a host of benefit plans—pension, insurance, profit-sharing, housing, and safety programs—that were aimed at winning employee loyalty. During this period industrial relations was predicated on the absence of the union, on creating a climate that would make labor organization unappealing to workers.[26]

The field acquired a major institutional base at the end of World War II as large state universities launched industrial relations programs, among them Cornell and the universities of Minnesota and California, all in 1945, and the University of Illinois in 1946. These programs brought together faculty from different departments—economics, psychology, sociology, law—to pursue research and teach in the area of labor-management relations.[27]

The New Deal and more decisively World War II made the union a central actor that the leaders of industrial relations could not ignore. The Wagner Act had given the trade union legal recognition and legitimacy. The organizing drives of the 1930s, however, did not lead inevitably to victories at the bargaining table. Contracts were slim documents that offered few fringe benefits and provided no union shop. Not until World War II were the foundations laid for a framework in which labor and management could resolve their conflicts.[28]

Detailed contracts were hammered out for the first time as employers and unions yielded to the momentum of a wartime economy and to the prodding of agencies, principally the War Labor Board. Bowing to Roosevelt's request for a no-strike pledge, many unions took their disputes with management to the Board, which helped the parties resolve their deadlocks. Not only did the Board help to write the first substantial negotiated agreements, but it also settled grievances. Pressure from Board neutrals led to the adoption of grievance arbitration clauses in contracts—agreements that workers' grievances would not be resolved by strikes, but by a process ending in a decision binding on both parties.[29]

Many of the influential figures who shaped the university industrial relations programs were labor economists who had worked on the staff of the War Labor Board. Clark Kerr, John

Dunlop, Robben Fleming, and others acquired skills through their wartime experience that they would use as the country's leading arbitrators.[30] Later, their flair for mediating the competing claims of interest groups won some of them top administrative posts at universities: George Schultz at Chicago, Dunlop at Harvard, Kerr at California, and Fleming at Michigan.[31]

Involvement with the War Labor Board undoubtedly colored their assumptions about the university's role in industrial relations. Their work taught them to look for common ground between the two antagonists. As neutrals, they felt an overriding commitment to a process of dispute settlement that would guarantee industrial stability and productivity. Unlike their predecessors in university industrial relations, they regarded the union as a legitimate institution. But it was not as labor's partisans that they built their reputation: The union was overshadowed in their discussions by an emphasis on the peace-making mechanism.

Pioneers in labor economics, such as Richard Ely, John Commons, George Barnett, and other institutionalists of the progressive period, represented a striking contrast to the War Board generation. Breaking away from the free-market view of the trade union as an unnatural constraint on the economy, these scholars advocated labor organization. Social reformers, they urged government intervention to protect workers through safety, minimum wage, and social security legislation. The institutionalists viewed unions as disenfranchised organizations; the founders of modern industrial relations assumed that labor already had a stake in the economic enterprise.[32]

The architects of the wartime industrial relations system feared that peacetime turbulence would rupture the bond that had formed between labor and management. The country's biggest strike wave, a walkout of 4.6 million workers in 1946 in the steel, mining, electrical, and other industries, signaled the growing labor insurgency. Economic controls were off, and workers were trying to stay even with the inflationary spiral.

The explosion of strikes convinced industrial relations experts that keener bargaining skills and more shared experiences between the two parties would have prevented these outbreaks. Hard-headed discussion between labor and management in a university setting would help to prevent discord and thereby contribute to "industrial peace" and greater productivity.

Apprehensions about labor strife also influenced the research priorities of the early industrial relations faculties. The most prominent areas of investigation were those into the roots of industrial peace.[33] Similar preoccupations have influenced the studies of labor's newest battleground, the public sector.[34]

Running through the rhetoric of industrial relations was the assumption that labor and management had common interests, interests that were clouded by a failure of communication. Charles Luckman, president of Lever Brothers, recommended that business raise a million dollars to finance college training for 500 business and labor officials. His recommendation typified this faith in knowledge as an instrument of labor-management harmony:

> We need to do a gigantic job of air-conditioning in labor relations. We need to sweep from our mind the cobwebs of ignorance. For we cannot get mutual understanding without mutual knowledge. We cannot get mutual knowledge without mutual education.[35]

Despite their efforts to strike a value-free tone, the promoters of industrial relations had definite social commitments. Their primary allegiance was to the stability of the economic order, in whose fruits labor and management could equally share. Edwin E. Witte, chairman of the Economics Department at the University of Wisconsin and the first president of the Industrial Relations Research Association, established in

1947, expressed his preference for a system in which traditional adversaries both gained by subordinating their interests to "the prosperity of industry and the general welfare":

> Clearly management must wholeheartedly accept unionism and recognize that workers can be loyal at one and the same time to the company and the union. . . . Unions must cease berating management, cooperate in trying to secure maximum production, and leave no doubt of their acceptance of our system of free enterprise.[36]

The views of industrial relations had their parallel in industrial social science, which gained an increasing following in corporations during World War II. These social scientists and their champions in the personnel departments also denied that industrial conflict was rooted in competing interests. They, too, held that discord could be remedied by improved communication. Psychologists influenced by the human relations school of Elton Mayo, who saw "a real identity between labor unrest and nervous breakdown," tried out strategies to raise workers' morale. They felt that this was the key to increased output. Using such methods as sociometry, industrial psychology, sociology, and the case method, a large number of corporations began training foremen, their first line of defense against labor dissension. Human relations courses also became an important part of the curriculum of schools of industrial relations.[37]

Unions countered that "human relations" was simply a more sophisticated technique to use to ensure a pliable work force. The UAW magazine *Ammunition* ran a cartoon that pictured a sign with the following statement from the Boss: "Even if we do cut your pay and break you down with speed up, we still love you."[38]

The new institutes gave the reigning philosophy of industrial peacemaking concrete expression. A liberal Republican legislature in New York State, whose majority leader, Irving Ives, became its first dean, established the first and most famous of these programs, the New York State School of Industrial and Labor Relations, at Cornell in 1945. Edmund Ezra Day, president of Cornell, summed up the vision of the school's founders:

> There are still those who think we are trying to produce more astute labor agitators. Nothing could be further from the truth. In a word, the aim of the School is to improve industrial and labor relations. This the School proposes to do by organizing and offering the means of more knowledge and better understanding among those in organized labor, management, and government who are likely to determine the course of industrial and labor relations in this country.[39]

Practically, this meant that schools of industrial and labor relations were squeamish about supporting separate labor programs responsible to their own client groups. An advisory board representing the interests of labor, management, and the public, it was felt, was sufficient to provide direction for all programs. It was as though the builders of these institutes wanted to transplant the War Labor Board framework, which had representatives from the same constituencies to the university. Joint classes and a common curriculum were the appropriate vehicles for building a cooperative spirit and teaching the intellectual tools uniting careers in business, government, and labor.

Labor needed no special faculty, since impartial professors could teach management and union representatives equally effectively. Those in the field would have agreed with the approach urged by Clarence J. Hicks, a pioneer and founder of the industrial relations section at Princeton:

> If the strong and weak points of an employer-employee relations and of trade unionism and of labor legislation are to be fairly and fearlessly studied, that work can be done only by those who are disinterested as well as competent, who have no selfish interests to serve, and who are trusted by all concerned.[40]

It was fitting that this faith in scholarly neutrality was enshrined in the name of the Industrial Relations Research Association. President Witte noted that the choice of "research" in the title was deliberate, it was done "to emphasize the impartial character of the organization and the purposes it serves."[41]

Labor Education's Challenge to Industrial Relations

Advocates of labor education tried to demolish industrial relations' claim that unionists could be trained in a disinterested manner. They argued that a program for workers should reflect the union's role as an interest group with goals often antagonistic to those of management. Mark Starr, former instructor at Brookwood and education director of the ILGWU and one of the most articulate exponents of this view, stated bluntly:

> The union leader must satisfy the expectation of his members by wage advances, and this may not coincide with the hopes of the shareholders for increased dividends. If the production pie can be made bigger, the cuts can be larger for both, but what if the pie shrinks owing to changes in methods, markets, or material? The coat and suit manufacturers can retire to Florida on his wartime profits, while his operators sadly apply for unemployment insurance.[42]

How, Starr asked, can you expect harmony in the classroom when labor and business are so often at odds in the marketplace? "When two armies fight, their strategies and tactics are not discussed in joint meetings."[43] Only when these two interest groups have met their respective educational needs, Starr asserted, would it be fruitful to bring them together.

Labor educators would always suspect that the impartial stance of industrial relations concealed a promanagement bias. Why else, the instinctive partisans assumed, would these academics extol a balance between two combatants so unequally matched. Labor educators would associate industrial relations with an obsession with labor peace, not with the eclectic interests expressed in studies like Seymour Lipset's on labor and American society, Walter Galenson's on international labor, and Arthur Ross's on wage determination.

Other critics noted that the priority given to industrial relations had taken the sting out of the labor curriculum. Irvine Kerrison, then director of the Rutgers labor program, surveyed labor courses conducted in 1949–50 and showed that only three dealt with political action and one with organizing. Few graduates of industrial relations schools were going to work with unions. Writing in 1951, Kerrison found that since 1935, only 36 out of 875 graduates had held union jobs.[44]

Labor educators wanted to dissociate their vocation from the field of industrial relations. At a conference of the American Labor Education Service on October 13, 1945, the attending educators contended that industrial relations courses should not be equated with "workers' education."[45]

The 1948 congressional hearings on proposed legislation to establish a Labor Extension Service, modeled after that in agriculture, forced the alliance of trade unionists and educators supporting the bill to marshal their broadest arguments in favor of labor education. The testimony supporting the bill, which would have given federal funds to colleges and universities to conduct noncredit training, embraced the contradictory positions of industrial relations and of interest-group politics. To reassure opponents of the legislation, its supporters tried to persuade them that the extension service would soften tensions between labor and management. Philip Murray, president of the CIO, said that a better trained union leadership would help stabilize labor relations: "When facts are once known and agreed to by both sides, more than half of the area of potential disagreement in industrial relations is eliminated."[46]

While trying to soothe the opposition with promises of industrial peace, the promoters of labor education were also contesting Senator H. Alexander Smith's (Republican, New Jersey) case for classes serving both labor and management. Smith proposed that management get the same services under the bill as labor.[47] Witnesses for the bill contended that workers were as entitled to services paid for with their tax dollars as the more powerful groups, which had reaped the most benefits. The training of union members was as appropriate for the state university to perform as was the grooming of students for management positions. They also insisted that labor had been shortchanged by the federal government, while farmers, a much smaller group in the work force, were receiving a bounty from the Agricultural Extension Service. Congress, they said, had never carried out the mandate of the Morrill Act to educate the "industrial classes."[48]

The analogy to agricultural extension is one that current advocates of federal support for labor education have drawn in their appeals.[49] J. C. Turner, president of the International Union of Operating Engineers, who was involved in drafting the legislation for the National Labor Extension Act, used this argument in a recent speech:

> "Some thirty years ago, as a Vice President of the Greater Washington Central Labor Union, I assisted in drafting proposed legislation that would have created a National Labor Education Extension Act. My recollection of the Morrill Act of 1862, the bedrock legislation for public post-secondary education, is that it was "to teach such branches of learning as are related to agriculture and the mechanic arts . . . in order to promote the liberal and practical education of the industrial classes. . . ."
> During the century or so since the state colleges began their steady growth, I have to assume that the ivy has grown over the words "mechanic arts" because the agricultural extension service exists as a model of continuing education, while not a penny of Federal money has been appropriated for labor extension education."[50]

Neither the conciliatory pleas nor the appeals to interest-group consciousness converted the staunch opponents of the bill, who saw in it all the marks of "class-conscious" or "anti-free enterprise" legislation. The coup de grace came when a General Motors employee, Adam K. Stricker, who had attended an economics course at the University of Michigan Labor Education Service, charged that the class was infested with left-wing bias. Stricker's testimony not only strengthened the hand of the opponents of the bill but also led to the regents closing down the Michigan Labor Program. It did not surface for almost a decade.[51]

The Contemporary Scene: From Extension to Credit

If university labor programs were to survive, they needed to establish their own unique institutional identity, attract a clientele they could count on for political support, and provide an ever-diversified array of services for this constituency. The history of the Rutgers University Labor Education Center, the most comprehensive labor institute, demonstrates all these ingredients at work. The program Rutgers built and the stages in which its various components developed illustrate the shape of university labor education today.[52]

The Institute for Management and Labor Relations was established by the New Jersey legislature in 1947 in the Extension School of Rutgers to carry out a characteristically industrial relations mission, its purpose being to promote

> harmony and cooperation between management and labor and greater understanding of industrial and labor relations, thereby to enhance the unity and welfare of the people of the state.[53]

An advisory committee with equal membership from labor, management, and the public oversaw three separate teaching programs aimed at each of these audiences. Despite the mystique of harmony this balanced representation was supposed to inspire, labor and management representatives quickly began sparring with each other. Before advisory committee meetings, each group often held their own caucus.

Arguments erupted among the institute faculty over the perennially explosive issue of separate versus joint classes.[54]

The labor education unit managed to create its own beach-head in the institute with a separate extension program of bread-and-butter short courses (six to eight weeks), conferences and institutes, and one-week summer schools tailored to the needs of an individual local or national union or aimed at an interunion group. The courses, which typically awarded a certificate for successful completion, used the drawing card of practical training in grievance handling, bargaining, public speaking, union administration, and other skills to attract middle-level leadership (shop stewards, committeemen) and officers.

As of 1955, the labor program had formed its own trade union consulting committee made up of influential leaders from individual unions and the state federation to advise the program and lobby for its interests in the state. In the advisory committee, the state university found a valuable ally that could use its political clout to steer higher-education budgets through the legislature.

The "tool" courses Rutgers initiated laid the foundation for a longer-term certificate program, the Union Leadership Academy started in 1956. The Labor center conceived the academy as a venture to deepen the interest that the shorter, more intensive courses had aroused. The academy offered interdisciplinary courses drawing on the social sciences (labor and politics, labor and society, labor and the economy) over a four-year period.

The style and content of long-term courses, which were developed at other labor centers as well, anticipated that of future degree programs. Academic faculty were frequently used and reading and writing assignments were given; the students were a mix from different unions. The perspective of the classes was more comprehensive than the ad hoc improvisations of many extension programs. Rather than providing a

group of unionists with practical solutions to immediate
organizational problems, such as how to handle grievances or
run a meeting, they placed the union's situation in a larger
setting, whether social, political, or historical.[55]

It was natural that once the interests of labor students were
whetted by taking a more general progression of classes, they
would seek degrees in labor studies. Pressures for the country's first undergraduate degree in the field came from Rutgers
students, who had completed short courses and long-term
certificate classes and who wanted to continue their studies.[56]

The B.A. in Labor Studies launched in 1967 by University
College, the Rutgers evening division, extended what Herbert
Levine called a "pathway of learning opportunities." Concentrations in labor in the master's and doctorate programs in
education, a master's in labor studies, and two-year degrees in
the field in the state's community colleges sprang up as
Rutgers struggled to widen its services.

The founding of the Labor College in New York City in
1971, another of the early degree programs (it awards both
associate and bachelor's degrees), also illustrated the decisive
role played by trade unionists in nondegree classes in the
establishment of labor studies degrees.[57] The first graduating
class of the two-year Labor–Liberal Arts program originated
by Cornell's labor education service pressed for a degree that
would enable them to continue their studies. Bernard Rosen-
berg, a member of Local 3 IBEW (International Brotherhood
of Electrical Workers) and one of the leaders of the student
group, explained its goals: "But after completing the two
years, we began asking: 'Is this the end of labor education for
us?' Why should our people be denied the opportunity to be
professionals?"[58]

The Labor College opened as a result of the political
support lent to their campaign by Harry Van Arsdale, the
powerful president of the New York City AFL-CIO Central
Labor Council. Van Arsdale won Rockefeller's support for
the idea, and his union donated and renovated a building.

After failing to persuade Cornell's School of Industrial and Labor Relations to start a degree, the graduates won the support of Empire State College, an experimental division of the State University of New York. Empire State gave advanced standing to labor–liberal arts graduates who wished to pursue a degree.

The equation of a labor–liberal arts certificate with credit toward a degree led to changes in that extension program. Cornell insisted that standards would have to be raised in labor–liberal arts if students were going to use it as a stepping-stone to college. Grades were required, the program was lengthened, and course materials were tightened and standardized. The program now put greater emphasis on college preparation than it did on training in union leadership techniques.[59]

The Labor Studies Boom

Labor programs in other industrial states with large concentrations of unionized workers charted a course like the one Rutgers pursued. Although the first wave of programs started after World War II, 50 percent of the universities and colleges in the UCLEA (University and College Labor Education Association), the professional organization in the field, were less than ten years old in 1976.[60] The association represents 47 institutions, mostly land-grant universities, in 28 states (some, like Michigan, have more than one labor program) as well as in Puerto Rico, Canada, and the District of Columbia. According to the most recent survey, the member programs have a staff of 335.[61] The number of staff ballooned during the 1970s—at Penn State and Ohio State it has tripled—and it would be even larger if it were not for the fiscal stringency of higher education. Extension instructors either work out of a main campus and travel around the state or run programs from a branch campus or regional office.[62]

Most frequently housed in the institute of industrial and

labor relations or the extension school, the labor centers usually work with an individual local union or with the district or regional groupings of locals in the same national union. In addition, labor centers sponsor interunion programs with local or state central bodies, the organizations in which the AFL-CIO has vested responsibility for education. Most university programs are tied to the labor hierarchy in their states through their advisory committees, which often include the officers of both state and city central bodies. Like Rutgers, many of these schools offer both traditional short courses and the long-term certificate programs.

The most recent development in the history of labor education is the explosion of degree programs in labor studies. The change has been startling. In 1965 there was one degree program, at the University of Massachusetts, while in a little more than a decade there were nine on the undergraduate and three on the graduate level. The degree curricula characteristically have a broader, more multidisciplinary approach than do the extension classes. Such courses as labor and politics, theories of the labor movement, labor economics, and labor law typically appear in their course offerings.[63]

One of the areas of most rapid growth for labor studies has been on community college campuses. In 1977 there were close to 40 two-year degrees in the field.[64] The United Auto Workers first encouraged this development in October 1967, when they tried to persuade community colleges in Detroit and Flint to start these programs. With funds from the Ford Foundation, the labor extension service at the University of California–Berkeley began a pilot project at Meritt College, a two-year school in Oakland, which was to have considerable influence. It constructed a degree in labor and urban studies to provide training particularly to minority trade unionists. Its example led to the development of labor studies degrees at community colleges throughout the Bay Area.

The creation of labor studies programs has enabled labor educators to upgrade their position in the universities. Attain-

ing standing as an academic discipline—having the authority
to grant credit, to provide faculty rank, to draw students with
a long-term commitment—is in part an attempt by labor
centers to slough off their second-class status as extension
programs.

Herbert Levine, director of the Rutgers labor program, was
one of the first labor educators to urge his colleagues to
improve their position in the university hierarchy:

> Once university labor education accepts the obligation of provid-
> ing opportunities for long-term study for individual trade union-
> ists, it can no longer accept its precariously based position in the
> academic community. It becomes necessary for university labor
> education services to establish centers of learning with an identi-
> fiable body of knowledge to transmit, a competent faculty,
> acknowledged source materials, a comprehensible method of
> teaching and research, and a student body of sufficient size to
> warrant the effort.
>
> Most university labor educators would like to hold the rank of
> professor in their respective faculties. This means academic and
> lay prestige, greater compensation (in most cases), tenure, and
> other benefits. It also means acceptance and respect for compe-
> tence in a specialized field of knowledge. To accomplish all this,
> all labor educators cannot be programmers, administrators, and
> emergency teachers. Some will have to approach their field of
> knowledge in a manner that approximates the approach of
> professors in other disciplines.[65]

As a result of the emergence of academic programs, labor
centers would now have to reconcile the growing professionalization with their commitment to informal learning. These
dilemmas were ones the builders of university extension at the
School for Workers could hardly have foreseen.

Notes

1. Some of the most valuable sources on the history of workers'
education are Lawrence Rogin and Marjorie Rachlin, *Labor Education in the
United States* (Washington, D.C.: National Institute of Labor Education,

1968), pp. 11–25; Theodore Brameld (ed.), *Workers' Education in the United States* (New York: Harper Brothers, 1941); Bert MacLeech, "Workers' Education in the United States" (Ph.D. dissertation, Harvard University, 1951); Lawrence Rogin, "How Far Have We Come in Labor Education?" in *The Labor Movement: A Reexamination* (Madison: University of Wisconsin, Industrial Relations Research Institute, 1967).

2. Among the most valuable sources on the Brookwood experiment are Nat Hentoff (ed.), *The Essays of A. J. Muste* (Indianapolis, Ind., Bobbs-Merrill, 1967), pp. 67–105; and James O. Morris, *Conflict Within the AFL: A Study of Craft Versus Industrial Unionism, 1901–1938* (Ithaca: Cornell University Press, 1958), pp. 86–124.

3. Hentoff, A. J. *Muste*, p. 94.

4. Morris, *Conflict Within the AFL*, p. 93.

5. Richard Dwyer, *Labor Education in the United States: An Annotated Bibliography* (Metuchen, N.J.: The Scarecrow Press, 1977), p. 2.

6. Ibid., p. 4.

7. Morris, *Conflict Within the AFL*, p. 92.

8. Ibid., p. 121. I am indebted to Morris's account, especially pp. 111–24, for my understanding of the Brookwood-AFL conflict.

9. Ibid., pp. 87–89, 123.

10. Ibid., pp. 89, 114, 123.

11. Ibid., p. 122.

12. Robert Ozanne, "The Wisconsin Idea in Workers' Education," in *School for Workers 35th Anniversary Papers* (Madison: The School for Workers, The University of Wisconsin, 1960), pp. 41–42.

13. Dwyer, *Labor Education*, p. 6.

14. Ozanne, "The Wisconsin Idea," pp. 41–42; MacLeech, *Workers' Education*, p. 233. See Rogin and Rachlin, *Labor Education in the United States*, p. 245, for reference to the "teachers training" carried on by the YWCA, as well as by the residential schools.

15. Dwyer, *Labor Education*, p. 167; Lois Gray, "The American Way in Labor Education," *Industrial Relations* 5, no. 2 (February 1966): 4.

16. MacLeech, *Workers' Education*, p. 312; Ernest E. Schwartztrauber, *Workers Education: A Wisconsin Experiment* (Madison: University of Wisconsin Press, 1942), pp. 45, 65.

17. Ozanne, "The Wisconsin Idea," p. 43.

18. Ibid., p. 42; Rogin and Rachlin, *Labor Education*, p. 20.

19. Ozanne, "The Wisconsin Idea," p. 42.

20. Schwartztrauber, *Workers Education*, pp. 62–63.

21. Commons's role is discussed further in Ozanne, "The Wisconsin Idea," pp. 41–42.

22. The quotation from the journal is found in Lawrence Cremin, *The Transformation of the School* (New York: Vintage, 1961), p. 167. See Richard Hofstadter and C. DeWitt Hardy, *The Development and Scope of Higher Education in the United States* (New York: Columbia University Press, 1952), pp. 46–48, for a discussion of the University of Wisconsin's ethic, as well as its service to agriculture.

23. For insights into the origins of industrial relations, I am particularly indebted to Richard E. Dwyer, Miles E. Galvin, and Simeon Larson, "Labor Studies: In Quest of Industrial Justice," *Labor Studies Journal* 2, no. 2 (Fall 1977): 95–131; and George Strauss and Peter Feuille, "Industrial Relations Research: A Critical Analysis," *Industrial Relations* 17, no. 3 (October 1978): 259–77.

24. Milton Derber, *Research in Labor Problems in the United States* (New York: Random House, 1967), pp. 7–8; Milton Derber, *The American Idea of Industrial Democracy* (Urbana: University of Illinois Press, 1970), p. 210.

25. David Brody, *Workers in Industrial America* (New York: Oxford University Press, 1980), p. 53.

26. For a penetrating discussion of industrial relations during the 1920s, see ibid., pp. 48–81.

27. Dwyer et al., "Labor Studies," p. 101.

28. Collective bargaining during World War II is discussed in David Brody, "The Emergence of Mass-Production Unionism," in John Braeman et al. (ed.), *Change and Continuity in Twentieth-Century America* (Columbus: Ohio Sate University Press, 1964), p. 259.

29. Dwyer et al., "Labor Studies," p. 105; Strauss and Feuille, "Industrial Relations Research," p. 262; R. W. Fleming, *The Labor Arbitration Process* (Urbana: University of Illinois Press, 1965), p. 15.

30. Dwyer et al., "Labor Studies," pp. 105–6; Strauss and Feuille, op. cit., p. 262; Jack Barbash, *Universities and Unions in Workers' Education* (New York: Harper Brothers, 1955), p. 8.

31. Dwyer et al., "Labor Studies," p. 112.

32. Strauss and Feuille, "Industrial Relations Research," pp. 260–62. See also George Strauss, "Directions in Industrial Relations Research," in Proceedings of the 1978 Annual Spring Meeting Industrial Relations Research Association, May 11–13, 1978, Los Angeles, California, pp. 531–36; Milton Derber, "Divergent Tendencies in Industrial Relations Research," *Industrial and Labor Relations Review* 17, no. 4 (July 1964): 608.

33. Derber, "Divergent Tendencies," p. 605.

34. Strauss and Feuille, "Industrial Relations Research," p. 269.

35. Quoted in Edmund Ezra Day, "The School at Cornell University," *Industrial and Labor Relations Review* 3, no. 2 (January 1950): 225.

36. Quoted in Dwyer et al., "Labor Studies," p. 106.

37. My point about the connection between industrial relations and social science has been shaped by a reading of Loren Baritz, *The Servants of Power* (Middletown, Conn.: Wesleyan University Press, 1960).

38. Ibid., p. 175.

39. Day, "The School at Cornell University," p. 225.

40. Quoted in *The Journal of Educational Sociology* 20, no. 8 (April 1947): 225.

41. Proceedings of First Annual Meeting Industrial Relations Research Association, Cleveland, Ohio, December 29–30, 1948, p. 4.

42. Mark Starr, "The Search for New Incentives," *Industrial and Labor Relations Review* 3, no. 2 (January 1950): 252.

43. Mark Starr, "Unions Look at Education in Industrial Relations," *The Journal of Educational Sociology* 20, no. 8 (April 1947): 500.

44. Irvine L. H. Kerrison, *Workers' Education at the University Level* (New Brunswick: Rutgers University Press, 1957), p. 26.

46. Quoted in Norman Eiger, "Toward a National Commitment to Workers' Education: The Rise and Fall of the Campaign to Establish a Labor Extension Service, 1942–1950," *Labor Studies Journal* 1, no. 2 (Fall 1976): 140. I have relied on Eiger's interesting narrative in my account of the struggle for a labor extension bill.

47. Ibid., p. 139.

48. Ibid., p. 141.

49. Leonard Woodcock, former president, UAW, made such a parallel in a statement prepared for the Third Annual Joint Labor Education Conference, Walter and May Reuther UAW Family Education Center, November 14, 1976, UAW Education Department pamphlet, 1977, p. 9.

50. J. C. Turner, "Labor and Continuing Education," speech to the Invitational Conference on Continuing Education, Manpower Policy and Lifelong Learning, January 10, 1977, p. 4.

51. Eiger, "Toward a National Commitment," pp. 142–47.

52. The development of the Rutgers labor program is told in Herbert Levine, "Union-University and Inter-University Cooperation in Workers' Education in the United States," in International Labor Office, *The Role of Universities in Workers Education* (Geneva: 1974, pp. 180–96.)

53. Ibid., p. 182.

54. Ibid., p. 183.

55. Rogin and Rachlin, *Labor Education*, pp. 169–82. See Frieda H. Goldman, (ed.), *Reorientation in Labor Education* (Chicago: The Center for the Study of Liberal Education for Adults, 1962), for an account of some of the pioneering ventures in marrying the perspective of the humanities to the study of labor.

56. Herbert Levine, "Union-University Cooperation in Labour Education," *Labour Education* no. 30 (April 1976): 29; and Levine, "*Union-University and Inter-University Cooperation,*" p. 176.

57. The background of the Labor College is told in Damon Stetson, "Union Members Broaden Their Vistas at Labor College Here," *New York Times*, September 4, 1972; "The ILR School's Labor Studies Certificate Program," report, Cornell New York State School of Industrial and Labor Relations, Metropolitan District, 1972, pp. 3–4.

58. Quoted in Stetson, "Union Members."

59. *Labor Studies Certificate Program*, p. 4.

60. The figures here were cited in the remarks of Dale Brickner, director of the Labor Program Service, Michigan State University, and then president of the University College Labor Education Association to the Joint Conference on Labor Education, Walter and May Reuther UAW Family Education Center, November 15, 1976.

61. *1980 University and College Labor Education Association Directory of Member Institutions and Professional Staff.*

62. The scope and growth of university labor education are detailed in John R. MacKenzie, draft chap., "Labor Education in the United States," 1977, pp. 4, 7.

63. The best survey of the expansion of university labor studies programs and the most useful data on them are in Lois Gray, "Labor Studies Credit and Degree Programs: A Growth Sector of Higher Education," *Labor Studies Journal* 1, no. 1 (May 1976): 34–51.

64. The figure on the number of community-college labor studies programs, the best available "guesstimate," comes from a conversation with William Abbott, then director of the Service Center for Community College-Labor Union Cooperation, American Association of Community and Junior Colleges, November 8, 1977.

65. Herbert A. Levine, "Will Labor Educators Meet Today's Challenges?" *Industrial Relations* 5, no. 2 (February 1966): 38–39.

2

The Development of a
Labor Studies Program:
A Case Study

The story of our efforts at Federal City College (now the University of the District of Columbia) to establish a degree program in labor studies illuminates in miniature many of the issues involved in the emergence of this new field. Federal City, which opened in 1968 as the nation's first urban college with land-grant status, was created because of the lack of inexpensive, publicly supported higher education in the nation's capital. In 1977 FCC merged with Washington's two other public colleges, the District of Columbia Teachers College and the Washington Technical Institute, to become the University of the District of Columbia. The university serves an almost entirely black student body, many of whom are working adults.

A university with many of the earmarks of a city agency, UDC is treated like another body of the city government. For every university official with budgetary or administrative authority, there is often a District staff member who must approve or double-check his decisions. Still hamstrung by the restrictions of Congress, its budget, once approved by the mayor and the City Council, must go with the rest of the city's requests to Congress for approval. Employees function under many of the same civil-service rules as their counterparts in the District government.

Spread throughout the District in classroom and office buildings, the UDC has colleges in such areas as business and public management, liberal and fine arts, education, and life sciences. Still basically a four-year college, it runs a modest graduate program, with its major emphasis on the master's degree in education, counseling, social work, library science, and city planning. The university does not offer graduate instruction in the liberal arts and social sciences.

The Labor Studies Center:
An Umbrella for Diverse Programs

The Labor Studies Center (originally established at American University in 1967) moved to Federal City and found a home in the Division of Community Education in 1971. Now based in the College of Education and Human Ecology, the center serves as an umbrella under which varied but complimentary activities of service to the labor movement are conducted. A hybrid, like many other university labor institutes, the center is equipped to carry on academic instruction, extension programs, and research. It is now in the process of developing a clearinghouse for labor education materials.

The various units are not tidy compartments, but they are fluid enough to allow the staff to concentrate on any one area and to participate in other center activities as well. For example, although my teaching responsibilities are primarily academic, I taught three noncredit classes during my first two years. The center is attuned to multiple constituencies—local and national unions, the AFL-CIO, District and federal agencies, university officials and departments—any or all of which may be bearing down on us at any one time. It frequently has less of the feel of a department than of the hothouse atmosphere of a "boiler room," to use an image of our director's. Unlike a typical department, the center cannot function in the confines of "semesters" and "academic years" and still keep up with the press of demands.

Many on the faculty and in administration were not sure whether we were a "center," a "department," or some other entity. Few had a model for a program that appeared to carry on contradictory functions. But it was the very versatility of the center concept that appealed to us. Unlike a department, we could not be easily typecast and forced into a narrow range of activities. It also often seemed as though the center did not exist on the school's organization chart. Memos passed us by, and requests for reports arrived the day before they were due. This was frequently to our advantage, permitting us to maneuver with a minimum of oversight.

Our location, like those of many labor centers, came about as much by accident as by design. The School of Education, whose first two deans had strong commitments to adult and nontraditional education, had been the most hospitable school to be in. If the leadership of the School of Education changed and a more conventional teacher-educator took the helm, we feared that we would be hemmed in. The restructuring of the university confronted us with a problem we had talked about but could no longer avoid. We had to decide where we wanted to be located in the new organization.

The Labor Studies Center did not fit neatly into any of the proposed divisions of the University. The College of Graduate Studies, for example, would overwhelm us with its exclusively academic programs, its lack of noncredit courses. Collisions with the business school reinforced our worries about being based in the proposed College of Business and Public Administration: Being located in this school might mean that our noncredit courses would be priced out of the average local union's reach. The University of Iowa's labor program, a part of its business school, had been forced to charge prohibitive rates for extension classes, rates comparable to those offered management groups.

In a proposal submitted to Wendell Russell, president of the Mount Vernon campus, and to Cleveland Dennard, president of the Van Ness campus, we argued that the Labor Studies Center should be organized as an independent institute outside the colleges of the new university but on an equal standing with them. Our mix of programs and unique relationship to a trade union constituency and to other units of the university required this special status. As an independent unit reporting directly to an academic vice-president or comparable university official, we would avoid the delays and red tape seemingly inherent in university decision making. This arrangement, the proposal stated, would equip the center to respond flexibly to the demands of an outside institution:

> The Labor Education program unit provides primarily non-credit conferences, seminars, and short courses on labor education subjects for trade unions. These programs are co-sponsored and jointly planned with union organizations, whether national, state, local. These same organizations supply the students for the programs. This unique aspect of the Center means that the University itself inter-faces on a continuing basis with another institution through the Labor Studies Center. This brings with it the need for flexibility, for exceptions to normal rules of administration, as the university does when it deals with students as individuals. The Center presently has its own UDC approved registration system for students in this category as well as administrative flexibility in handling finances through the use of its D.C. Government Trust Accounts. Moreover, the Center needs to be able to respond swiftly and flexibly to the swiftly changing educational needs of its union constituency. An extension division cannot operate in a rigid framework.[1]

Unions frequently gave us only two weeks to plan a

program to prepare a bargaining team or a new group of stewards. The semester time frame could not easily accommodate the crisis atmosphere of the trade union, a mood produced by organizing campaigns, elections, and strikes. The unpredicted often forced changes and alterations in extension programs previously agreed on by union and university.

It was a common assumption among university labor center directors that their access to the president be the quickest possible, usually no more than two administrative steps away. The center sought such an arrangement to accelerate decision making, to get quick rulings in areas where only the top university official had the authority to make them. A labor center's relationship to the top leadership of the local, state, or national labor movement is strengthened if its director has such a direct tie to the university president. Those programs that require the official blessing of the university, the presence of senior administrators, for example, are in a strategic position to get it. Moreover, since labor centers often help to marshal union support for colleges and universities in city councils and state legislatures, their directors expect the ready ear of the president.

By not being submerged in an incompatible school, we would heighten our own identity. As an independent unit, we expected that we could bargain more effectively with other schools and departments in the university and that they would be more comfortable with us. We could more easily offer courses geared to the interests of students in other fields and expect their departments to open their classes to our students. With an organizational structure like the one we recommended, the University of Massachusetts Labor Studies program has offered electives to students from social work, education, and nursing. This arrangement might also help us forge ties with faculty from other departments who could teach a class in our program or crosslist one of their courses with us.

THE STAFF

The center's staff consists of a director, an assistant director, two full-time faculty members (myself and Isadore Goldberg), a secretary, an administrative assistant, and a host of part-time teachers who teach mostly noncredit short courses. The director, John MacKenzie, acquired much of his labor experience in union work in both the public and private sectors. He went through the program at the ILGWU (International Ladies Garment Workers Union) staff-training institute and then worked as an international representative for that union. His responsibilities for the union included leading strikes, running organizing campaigns, and negotiating with companies. His union career in the South led to his election as president of the Southwestern Virginia Central Labor Council. His next job as director of the Illinois State Employees' Council for AFSCME taught him skills in representing government workers. From AFSCME he moved to West Virginia University as assistant director of its labor program. He came to Washington to direct the labor institute at American University, and when the program moved to Federal City, he continued in the same position.

In addition to his administrative duties, MacKenzie attends to the political tasks that protect our flanks both inside and outside of the university. He acts as a buffer between the center and university administrators, deans, and department chairmen. (He reports directly to the dean of the School of Education.) His position as associate professor of Labor Studies and as chairman of the Academic Policy Committee of the Graduate School, which approves new courses and degrees, gives him additional academic credibility.

MacKenzie assiduously maintains the contacts between our institute and the Greater Washington Central Labor Council, the AFL-CIO, and individual local and national unions that

provide us with a political base in the city. We would turn to
these groups for support in expanding our program (such as in
securing a larger budget) or for help if the center's existence
were ever in jeopardy. Like many directors of labor centers,
MacKenzie solidifies ties between the university and the local
and national labor movement by advising its leadership on
educational, political, and administrative problems. He serves
as chairman of the Education Committee of the Greater
Washington Central Labor Council and has advised the
Maryland State Federation on educational matters. He has
also served as president of the University and College Labor
Education Association (UCLEA), the professional association
in the field.

During my years with the center, two former trade unionists have overseen our extension program. The first, William
Abbott, former education director of the United Rubber
Workers, came to Washington from Hawaii, where he had
worked for the Labor-Management Education Program of the
University and had served as the executive secretary of the
Hawaii Federation of College Teachers (AFT). Currently, the
assistant director is Edgar Lee, who had held union leadership
positions in the public sector. Lee had been assistant director
of the Education Department of the American Federation of
Government Employees (AFGE), the largest union representing federal government workers, and of the American Federation of State, County, and Municipal Employees (AFSCME).

THE PROGRAMS

The requests for training that come from the region's concentration of unions, without any direct promotion on our part,
are more than our small staff can handle. The center has
continually, but with little success, requested funds for more
staff to respond to the demands of the more than 210,000
union members and their local and district organizations in
the Greater Washington area. The Greater Washington Cen-

tral Labor Council has more than 110 local unions affiliated with it. The city is unique in that many of the locals' parent unions, the internationals, are headquartered here and consequently are more closely watched than they are in most labor towns.

The AFL-CIO and approximately 50 national and international unions are based in the District.[2] The center's program reflects the distinctiveness of the area's work force, a rich mixture of government, service, building and printing trades, and office workers.[3]

The city's labor unions include both settled and established labor organizations, as well as newly organized ones that are more exuberant and impatient. In a stewards' training course, I had students who were roofers, clerical workers (some of whom worked for unions), hospital workers from St. Elizabeth's Hospital, a federal installation, and Department of Labor employees. The roofers marveled at the comfortable conditions in the federal government (the construction workers had no "leave"—if they didn't work, they weren't paid) and were amazed that others would not casually walk off the job if they had a grievance.

The relatively high level of educational attainment of the city's work force is largely the result of the presence of the federal government, for which 56 percent of the employees work. One of the most rapidly growing areas of unionization today, the federal government has a greater proportion of organized workers than the work force as a whole. A larger proportion of workers here than in most cities has completed high school; many view education as a stepping-stone to better pay or to a more attractive job and often receive incentives from employers (such as tuition reimbursements) in their quest for upward mobility.

Much of our extension teaching is done with the youthful, rapidly expanding public sector and service employee locals. As locals win elections, struggle with the tasks of organizing and administering an unfamiliar structure, or prepare to handle an avalanche of grievances, they are apt to call on the center for help. Among our most frequent clients are locals of AFSCME, AFGE, APWU (American Postal Workers Union), and SEIU (Service Employees International Union).

We ran a "union administration" course for the officers and executive board of the AFSCME local, which had won an election to represent GS (General Schedule) and administrative employees at the college and had recently signed their first contract. Union administration and steward's training programs were conducted for a new local of the SEIU representing employees at the Washington Hospital Center. I taught two classes for officers and members of the Executive Board of AFSCME Local 2095 at St. Elizabeth's Hospital who were preparing to renegotiate their contract. The classes centered on understanding the legal framework of negotiations in the federal sector (particularly on interpreting what areas fell within the scope of bargaining) and on strengthening key provisions of their first agreement.

The Labor Studies Center may also develop a program for a national union. In the spring of 1976 we ran a conference in cooperation with the Education and Research Department of the APWU for officers and state representatives with educational responsibilities. The institute, conducted at the George Meany Labor Studies Center in Silver Spring, Maryland, acquainted the union leaders with teaching techniques, new content areas, and materials they could use in their work. The format, whether conference, short course, or institute, and its length, cost, location, and content vary with the preference of the union. These matters are typically worked out in planning sessions between the center's staff and the representatives of the unions.

In addition to providing training specially tailored for an individual union, the center twice a year cosponsors general courses, usually six to eight weeks in length, with the Greater Washington Central Labor Council. These are attended by members of a variety of local unions. The council assists in publicizing these classes, and we staff them. The most popular course, usually offered every cycle, is steward's training. This course in local union leadership skills and the art of grievance handling has a consistently large audience because of the constant turnover of these officials and the consequent need of inexperienced men and women to learn the basics of enforcing the contract. Other classes have been given in public speaking and parliamentary procedure, labor history, union administration (Building the Union), and arbitration. We have aimed courses at local union staff (business agents, for example) on the new pension law and on the use of economic data in collective bargaining.

The extension program has won remarkable independence from the university in carrying on its classes. Course topics, costs, schedules, and locations are worked out with relatively little interference from the administration. We even have our own admissions, registration, and attendance procedures. Students who meet the attendance requirements are awarded a certificate at the final class, and their achievement is noted on a university transcript. The certificate has special meaning for trade unionists who have never been to college. One union staffer who attended one of my courses had his certificate hanging prominently on his office wall.

The center also envisions public managers, particularly those with labor relations responsibilities, as part of its constituency. Partly at the urging of public-employee union leaders, who have been confronted with inexperienced management in the day-to-day rough and tumble of labor relations or across the bargaining table, MacKenzie decided that we should train municipal, state, and federal officials. He felt that courses for managers would improve the quality of labor relations in the public sector, where the law and regulations shaping unit determination (such as what employees the union is permitted to represent), bargaining, and dispute settlement are new and are undergoing rapid change.

One experiment in this form of training was the program

the Labor Studies Center conducted for both the management bargaining teams of Federal City College and D. C. Teachers College and the representatives of the faculty and staff unions, NEA (National Education Association) and AFSCME, respectively, at these institutions. The training concentrated on the skills both sides would need in negotiating their first contract.

The newest venture of the center, which flows directly from its commitment to extension, is the establishment of a National Labor Education Materials and Information Center. We house and will expand the collection of labor education materials (such as course outlines for short courses, conferences, institutes, summer schools) produced by unions, universities, and government agencies, nationally and internationally, which were originally gathered by the National Institute of Labor Education. The materials unit will collect additional materials, organize and catalog the collection, and provide information about its use. Instead of having to improvise a course outline every time a new topic arises, a union or university educator will have a handy reference for drawing on the ideas developed by other teachers.

My primary responsibility with the center has been with its academic unit, with the administration and teaching of the Labor Education concentration we offer through the Adult Education Department's master's degree program and the planning for a master's degree in Labor Studies. I coordinate the six courses (Theory, Structure, History, and Development of the Labor Movement; Labor Relations and Collective Bargaining; Labor Law; Labor Education and Administration in the United States) that offer graduate students in Adult Education an opportunity to specialize in the labor field. Our concentration supplements the teacher-training format of the required adult education curriculum—with its emphasis on "methods" and "techniques"—with the course material of labor studies.

These courses have attracted public school and college

teachers, some of whom are union members, government workers, labor relations and personnel officers, union officials, and an assortment of students who are taking the courses as electives. We have set up internships in labor education programs conducted by the center so that students in this specialty can learn more of the craft. One student, a former AFSCME official and now a government labor-relations officer, taught steward's training in the program we sponsor with the Central Labor Council. Another, an employee of the Library of Congress, taught a class to new stewards of SEIU Local 82 at their union hall.

Although we planned to continue these classes, much of our energies went into developing our own graduate degree, which, we hoped, would widen the reach of the center and meet a need that was not fulfilled by any other institution. Like other university labor programs, we were dissatisfied with playing an ancillary role in another department's degree. We yearned to shape our own curriculum, set our own requirements, and teach students whom we would select.

During my first two years at the Labor Studies Center, from 1975 to 1977, I spent much of my time working, particularly with MacKenzie, on planning the degree, conceptualizing the program, and helping guide it through the maze of committees and bodies that have jurisdiction over new offerings. I had much of the responsibility for drafting and redrafting our proposal.

The Master's Degree in Labor Studies: Its Conception

Our proposal was rooted in our perceptions of the center's strategic location in the nation's capital and of the constituencies we were uniquely equipped to attract by virtue of that location. The concentration of unions and federal agencies was an asset of no other university labor program. As MacKenzie once said to me, our position in Washington put us in the "catbird seat."

A graduate degree program shaped to this audience would distinguish our offerings from those of most labor centers in the industrial states. As we stated in our proposal:

> The majority of labor studies programs have not constructed an in-depth curriculum geared to the unique concerns of government workers. Their classes are still heavily weighted toward services to union members in the mass industries, e.g., steel, auto, chemical, rubber. A substantial public sector program would strengthen FCC's program both locally and nationally.[4]

The degree, whose centerpieces are training in trade union administration and public-sector labor-management relations, was one, we felt, no other institution in the Washington area was as well prepared to mount. The only other labor center in the area was the George Meany Center for Labor Studies in Silver Spring, Maryland, which ran a primarily noncredit staff-training program for officials of the AFL-CIO's member unions and awarded an undergraduate external degree (with Antioch College in Ohio) in labor studies. The industrial relations courses available at other institutions were heavily oriented toward private industry, emphasizing personnel, rather than the role of unions.

If our degree was approved, we expected to stand out nationally as well, since only two other universities (Rutgers and the University of Massachusetts at Amherst) were running master's programs in the field (no doctorate in labor studies as distinct from industrial relations is currently awarded). These were opportunities we could capitalize on, but we were apprehensive that other institutions might start their own degree if we did not act swiftly enough. A rumor that Cornell's School of Industrial and Labor Relations had applied for permission to establish a degree in the District drove us into a nervous frenzy.

Among the most important constituencies we were counting on were the officers and staff of local and national unions—presidents, secretary-treasurers, business agents, international representatives, and national union staff in such areas as public relations, research, health and safety, community services, bargaining, and legislation. These were the people whom MacKenzie called the "labor pros." A large number of these officials, we felt, would probably come from public-sector unions, which were most eager to learn the nuts and bolts of law, bargaining, union administration, and contract enforcement and had the least tradition to fall back on. The national headquarters of most of these unions are in Washington.

Our proposal underscored the advantages Federal City had in constructing a program that would appeal to this group:

> Federal City College's location at the center of the largest concentration of public employees in the country makes it ideally suited to offer training in public sector labor-management relations. As one of the early consultants involved in the planning of the Master's degree, Prof. Harvey Friedman, who directs the nation's oldest graduate programs in labor studies at the University of Massachusetts, put it: "With the expansion of public sector collective bargaining, particularly in the past four years, based on Executive Orders 10988, 11491, and 11616 and subsidiary executive orders, upon the Postal Reorganization Act of 1970 and upon the acceptance/tolerance of bargaining at the municipal level, a need for education in this important field has become obvious. Certainly the action in labor relations is in the public sector, and certainly the District of Columbia is in the center of action."[5]

Among the public-employee unionists most likely to benefit from the degree, the dominant group would certainly be from federal unions, such as AFGE, NTEU (National Treasury Employees Union), and APWU. Arthur Kane, then education director of the AFGE and former associate director of the Labor Studies Center, remarked at a staff meeting that federal labor relations was the "name of the game" in D.C. Further education might give them a leg up in their current jobs or give them an advantage in finding a better post. Union representatives in the federal sector often are at a loss in making sense of the peculiarities of the law and regulations under which they must function. While the federal government showers money on management for labor relations bargaining, unions in the public sector must fend for themselves. In a speech to the Society of Federal Labor Relations Professionals, Kane made a telling argument for the need for federal union training needs:

> in federal labor relations training and functions, all funds are for Federal supervisors and managers. Many millions of dollars are channeled in these training endeavors. The Labor Relations Training Center of the U.S. Civil Service Commission prepares programs for management personnel of all agencies. . . .
>
> In addition, each federal agency provides Labor Relations Management Training for its own staff. They also work with the Civil Service Commission by sending managerial representatives for a broad range of training needs. Agencies also work with Universities/Colleges—on programs written for Management personnel. For all these activities administrative leave and Per Diem are provided to managers and supervisors for training at public expense.[6]

MacKenzie expected the degree, particularly in the beginning, to attract a large number of public managers—from local, state, and county agencies, but particularly from the federal government. Federal bureaucrats, a group with a keen appreciation for the value of every additional bit of certification in their "personnel jackets," would no doubt use the program to advance themselves. Labor relations jobs, once held in low esteem, now are accorded higher status and pay on the civil-service ladder. Personnel officers were under intense pressure to increase their knowledge of labor relations.

The U.S. Civil Service Commission had stipulated that all personnel officers "must have, or promptly obtain after entry on duty, appropriate labor management relations skills and maintain such skills on a continuing basis." Among the areas that these officials were expected to master were:

> Knowledge of laws, executive orders, regulations, policies, and
> concepts pertaining to Federal labor-management relations;
> Knowledge of current issues, practices, and precedents in labor-
> management relations; Ability to establish and maintain effective
> work relationships with both local and national representatives of
> unions, with full consideration of the bilateral nature of labor-
> management relations.[7]

We expected another contingent of students to come from
recent college graduates whose commitment to social action
made a trade union career or one in labor education an
attractive one. We planned to rely on internships with unions
and government agencies to give them some practical season-
ing and to offer potential employers a chance to look them
over.

One of the underlying assumptions behind the degree was
that the job market for people with labor studies skills was
expanding and that it had multiple career paths. In our
proposal we argued:

> There is no surplus of people with labor studies skills on the job
> market since the demand for trained professionals in the field is
> such a burgeoning one. . . . Graduates of our Masters program
> will have a competitive edge in securing new jobs or in moving up
> to a more attractive position in their current institution.[8]

Among the jobs we stated our program could prepare for
were: (1) union staff positions on the local, regional, and
international levels; (2) teaching jobs in labor studies programs
in colleges and universities, particularly at the community
college level; (3) posts in manpower and community service
agencies; and (4) labor relations, personnel, and training jobs
with federal, city, state, and county agencies.

We were optimistic about the program's ability to place its
graduates. If Harvey Friedman, director of the University of
Massachusetts labor program, could put together probably
the best track record of any graduate program at his univer-

sity, partly by placing graduates in unions and federal agencies in Washington, we should be able to do at least as well.

We designed a core of courses in the degree that all students would be expected to take, whatever their area of specialization. These required courses, including such standards as Labor Law, Theories of the Labor Movement, and Labor and the American Economy, came closest to being the kernel of our infant discipline. As the framework for any more intense study in the field, they would knit together what might otherwise be a fragmented program.

A student concentrating in trade union administration would be expected to take such courses as Labor and Politics and Collective Bargaining, classes that suggest the multi-faceted role of the trade union official. He could delve into electives like Pensions and Fringe Benefits, Health and Safety, and Arbitration and Dispute Settlement, all of which flow from the bargaining and grievance-handling responsibilities of a union job.

The public sector option similarly illuminates our assumptions about the degree's constituency. In addition to such general courses as Public Sector Collective Bargaining and Dispute Settlement, we planned to offer technical training geared to the federal sector through a course such as The Federal Budget Process and Wage Administration. We also envisioned the program providing courses for students in other disciplines who were preparing for jobs in fields—e.g. teaching and nursing—that had recently been unionized. Our proposal featured courses such as Teachers and Collective Bargaining and Labor Relations and the Health Services.

We wanted our program to be flexible enough to accommodate a mix of students with different expectations. Because our constituency was made up of union and government officials, we also expected to have a more racially diverse group of students than that in the university as a whole. We looked forward to attracting full-time students as well as a substantial number of others, such as those in mid-career, who would be interested in taking only a limited number of courses. Federal City had only recently (in January 1977) begun to admit "nondegree" students, largely as the result of a proposal of MacKenzie's and mine to the Academic Policy Committee of the Graduate School, the committee he chaired. At that time, FCC was unique among the District's colleges and universities in not having a policy to tap the large market of part-time students in the area, including the many government workers. Such a policy, we believed, would be crucial to the success of our master's degree.

THE STRUGGLE FOR APPROVAL

The most careful conceptualizing of the degree and the tightest arguments for its necessity were not sufficient to win its adoption. We had to run a gauntlet of college committees and respond to their faculty members whose preoccupations differed sharply from our own. We were forced to shape our degree proposal to meet the conflicting and often overlapping guidelines of the School of Education Curriculum Committee, the Graduate School, and the Faculty Senate. We needed the approval of the provost, the president, and the Board of Higher Education as well. In the course of a year's transactions with approval bodies, we had to tailor, refine, and revise our proposal and strategy in order to answer their questions and mollify their anxieties. More positively, the doubts raised by some committee members pushed us to sharpen the definition of the degree and its relationship to the overall program of the Labor Studies Center.

The degree approval guidelines and objections raised by the committees forced us to present the degree in a format with which the typical faculty member would be comfortable. In the process our proposal took on a symmetry that our confusion and ambivalence belied. Sample syllabi, course descriptions, a catalog statement, a budget, model programs, and degree requirements all gave the proposal the necessary academic polish. We were queried about prerequisites and admissions requirements, pressed about the absence of a research-skills course (we added courses in statistics and research), and asked to be more precise about the total number of credits in the degree.[9]

One vocal committee member, the chairperson of one of the graduate departments, sounded us out about aliens in the job market and about municipal unions as the cause of urban bankruptcy. Probably expressing the apprehensions of many of his colleagues, a professor sitting on the Academic Policy Committee of the Graduate School urged that our degree have all the academic "trappings." This was necessary, he said, because it was the first graduate degree, prepared under the new guidelines, that the board of trustees would look at.

Like the developers of any new program, we staked out our own territory in order to avoid incursion by other departments that might claim the field as their own. Although this task was not as formidable as it would be in a university with a full-fledged graduate school and a powerful social-science department, it was nonetheless a tense one. MacKenzie, who once described the university as a collection of warring "building trades units," had premonitions of future conflicts.

Before confronting any committees, we scrupulously titled our courses in order to avoid disputes with other disciplines: Organizational Psychology became Labor Leadership Development; Sociology of the Work Place became Labor and the Community. Anticipating a quarrel with the Business School, MacKenzie insisted that we call our introductory course Introduction to Labor Studies rather than Introduction to Labor Relations. The latter course was one that they might claim because of its affinity with industrial relations, a discipline they wanted to preempt. He also feared that if we did not launch our degree rapidly the business school would encroach even further on our domain.

As we made our first appearance defending our proposal before the committees, his fears were confirmed. The questioning from the Academic Policy Committee, he observed, made him feel like a stranger to the guild being sized up by a group of building tradesmen. What uniquely qualified the Labor Studies Center to teach this collection of courses? a member of another committee asked us. Wasn't this the job of business schools and law schools?

Predictably, the business school began to snipe at us through its representative on the Graduate Council, the body composed of the chairpersons of all graduate departments. The business school offered a few labor courses in its undergraduate curriculum that had a definite promanagement stamp on them. The catalog description of the topics to be covered in the labor law class read like an invitation to study union-busting tactics: "the doctrine of criminal conspiracy; the injunction as an anti-labor weapon; modern applications of the anti-trust laws to limit union power; modern legal limitation on the right to strike; picketing as a coercive force and picketing as an example of free speech."[10]

Ironically, it was our proposal to do public-sector training that had rankled some of the business school faculty. The school, whose official name was the School of Business and Public Management, had been planning to introduce a graduate degree in public management, but it had not submitted a proposal for it.

After a deceptively tranquil beginning, the business school spokesman went on the attack in the Graduate Council meeting. Wouldn't our projected classes duplicate some of those already being offered by his school? Furthermore, he contended, training in the labor relations of the public sector was an extremely "narrow" part of "personnel administration," the sphere of the business school. This limited specialty hardly warranted coverage in a separate degree, he said.[11]

These points were but a mild prelude to what appeared to

be his real agenda. He suggested that we consider conducting our program jointly with the business school. An ally of his on the committee, a professor who had had some training in industrial psychology, questioned the rationale for the center's location in the School of Education, rather than in a school with an "industrial" orientation.[12]

MacKenzie joined the issue by arguing the distinctiveness of our work and the concomitant need for the program's autonomy. Labor studies, he said, was different from industrial relations. From the vantage point of industrial relations, labor was a "problem" of business. I later added that industrial relations programs rarely dealt with the concerns of public employees.[13]

Invoking the record of past skirmishes between labor and management in schools of business and industrial relations institutes, MacKenzie asserted that labor would be a junior partner in any such joint enterprise. He extended an offer of cooperation to the business school representative, but it was an invitation that presumed our own firm and independent base. Labor Studies would consider opening our courses to their students, he said, and we hoped they would reciprocate. Despite the criticisms leveled at us, our degree slid through by a narrow vote.[14]

In time, we learned more about the basis of the business school's objection to our degree. We discovered that the inclusion of public managers as one of our projected constituencies had triggered anxieties in some of its representatives. A memo written by an industrial relations specialist on their faculty at the academic dean's request criticized the broad sweep of our degree:

> Does the proposed degree aim at training potential students for managerial and supervisory positions in government or private firms? If so, is this one of the objectives of the Labor Studies Center? Wouldn't this be an attempt to compete with or duplicate some of the programs and course offerings of the *School of Business*

and Public Management? Was the Labor Studies Center established to train personnel and labor relations specialists and managerial personnel?[15]

Instead of a master's in labor studies, he recommended that the center offer a degree in personnel administration and labor relations jointly with the business school. The thrust of his proposal was that business faculty would concentrate on two areas, (1) public personnel and (2) labor relations and personnel management in the private sector, and we would handle courses dealing directly with trade union administration. A labor studies degree, he said, would be a handicap for many students in their search for jobs:

> From the standpoint of securing jobs or advancing their careers, students would be better off with a degree in Personnel and Labor Relations from a School of Business and Public Administration. A degree in Labor Studies would not have as great an appeal; it would be too specialized and too narrow to appeal to personnel specialists, supervisors who represent and are part of management in the negotiation and administration of collective bargaining agreements, and students who intend to work in private or public personnel departments.[16]

Our skirmishes with the business school were not over. Our proposal had gone from the Graduate Council to the provost's office, and was now in the hands of the Educational Policy Committee of the Faculty Senate. MacKenzie and I appeared before this committee, answered a few brief questions, and left assuming the degree had sailed through. Shortly thereafter we learned from the committee chairman that one of the members not present at the meeting, a business school professor associated with the public management program, had some doubts about the degree. When I spoke to him, I discovered that he was anxious about some of the course titles we had used in our public-sector concentration. Such titles as "Position Classification" and "Civil Service and Personnel Administration" caught his eye. These were subjects, he felt, that appropriately fell under the jurisdiction of the public management program. If we successfully laid claim to them, the projected master's degree in public administration would be endangered.

I felt that the business school was still probing our defenses, testing us to see on what positions we might yield. As we plotted our strategy, we determined not to cave in lest the business school then be encouraged to take control of the whole program.

MacKenzie and I negotiated our position with four business school representatives. There was the expected ideological jousting as both sides staked out claims to the subject matter of the labor courses. At one point, I said that it was ironic to be lectured for poaching by a discipline (public administration) that all too recently political science considered to be an upstart. This was all beside the point. Logical distinctions would not quiet the business school's fears that we loomed as a rival for the same pool of students.[17]

One business professor urged us to confine our recruiting to union officials, not managers. While continuing to insist on our own identity, we again made peace offerings and invited business students to take our courses. In an effort to dispel any illusions of a joint degree, MacKenzie said that a business school credential would damage a graduate's chance of getting a job in the labor movement.[18] (At this writing, almost two years from the time the degree was ultimately approved, conflicts between the Labor Studies Center and the business school have erupted again. The acting dean of the College of Education proposed that our center be moved to the business school; we succeeded in changing this recommendation.)

We conceded that we would make our titles sufficiently precise so that there would be no confusion as to whose program they belonged. After consulting with our federal-sector adviser, Arthur Kane, we decided on modest changes. We changed Position Classification to Labor Relations and Position Classification and Civil Service and Personnel Administration to Labor Relations' Impact on Federal Personnel Administration. Apparently remembering his own experiences sparring with management, MacKenzie quipped that the business professors' manner was that of "father knows best."

When we attended the next meeting of the Educational Policy Committee, we showed the business professor our handiwork. He was delighted with the title changes and raised no objections when asked his opinion on the degree proposal. The way was cleared for the committee to approve the degree and to send it on to the Faculty Senate as a whole for consideration. The Senate approved the degree on April 1, 1977, and the Board of Trustees passed it on September 21, 1978.

Notes

1. *Memorandum*, To: Dr. Wendell P. Russell, President, Mount Vernon Campus, University of the District of Columbia, Dr. Cleveland Dennard, President, Van Ness Campus, UDC. From: John R. MacKenzie, Associate Professor and Director. Subject: Location of the Labor Studies Center within the Organizational Structure of the University of the District of Columbia, May 10, 1977, pp. 1–2.

2. We cite this figure as part of our argument for a master's degree in "Proposal for a Master's Degree in Labor Studies," submitted by Labor Studies Center, School of Education, Federal City College, 1976 (revised 1977), p. 1.

3. For a succinct description of the Washington labor movement, see Labor Studies Center Annual Report 1971, Division of Community Education, Federal City College, pp. 3–4. Evidence on the labor groups the center services can be found in the Annual Report, July 1, 1975, to June 30, 1976, Labor Studies Center, School of Education, Federal City College, pp. 1–4 (Labor Education Unit), and Appendix, pp. 2–3. *Memorandum*, from Edgar Lee to Jack MacKenzie, February 28, 1977, pp. 1–2, on "Listing of Course Activity," provides a sense of the breadth of the center's educational programs.

4. "Proposal," p. 8.

5. Ibid., p. 7.

6. Address by Arthur Kane to Society of Federal Labor Relations Professionals, February 25, 1977, pp. 2–3.

7. FPM Letter No. 250–3, Subject: Labor Management Relations Skills for New Personnel Officers, September 20, 1973, p. 2.

8. "Proposal," p. 15.

9. We drew up our proposal according to the specifications of *Guidelines for Development and Approval of Graduate Degree Programs at Federal City College*, 1976. For examples of the kinds of issues raised by the committees, see *Memorandum*, to Dr. John Jenkins, Dean, School of Education. From: Dr. Thomas John, Chairman, School of Education Curriculum Committee. Subject: Review of Labor Studies and Special Education Master's Degree Programs, June 16, 1977, pp. 1–2; The Graduate Academic Affairs Committee, "Minutes," September 2, 1976, pp. 1–2.

10. *Federal City College School of Business and Public Management. Catalog 1975–76*, Washington, D.C., p. 45.

11. Notes on Graduate Council meeting, October 18, 1976.

12. Ibid.

13. Ibid.

14. Ibid.

15. "Comments on the Proposal for a Master of Arts Degree in Labor Studies," n.d., p. 1.

16. Ibid., p. 2.

17. Notes on meeting between MacKenzie and Denker and business school representatives, March 14, 1977.

18. Ibid.

3

The Making of a Discipline: Labor Studies and the Quest for Academic Status

Throughout the campaign to establish our degree program, we felt compelled to clarify our field to an audience of often mystified academics. Did labor studies have a body of knowledge in its own right or was it merely an offshoot of one of the established disciplines? Would it have to be satisfied with borrowing from other, related fields—labor economics, industrial psychology, sociology—with what former UCLEA president Dale Brickner of Michigan State called the "cut and paste" approach?[1] We were wrestling with the issue that was unsettling many of our colleagues in labor programs throughout the country. It was not a dilemma unique to labor studies: Older fields had also waged a battle for academic autonomy. As late as 1920, sociology and political science were locked within departments of economics and history.[2]

Drawing the boundaries of this emerging field has been an integral part of its promoters' drive for academic recognition.

Tucked away in an extension division, labor educators rarely faced this pressure. Ad hoc programs posed no real threat to the established departments. In its pursuit of departmental status and degree-granting authority, labor studies needed a trademark to distinguish it from its rivals. Like any new field, labor studies touted and often exaggerated its uniqueness. In our degree proposal we engaged in the usual muscle flexing:

> The underlying assumption of our degree is that labor studies is an academic discipline in its own right, not a field that must depend solely for its nourishment on other departments. Labor studies has a unique core of knowledge, the study of the trade union and its multifaceted roles as well as its relationship to American culture and the rest of the world. [3]

The proliferation of labor studies programs, notably at the community college level, has made university labor educators even more determined to close ranks behind a definition of the field. In the absence of such a definition, it was feared, labor studies could easily be embraced by groups with different objectives. At a conference on community college labor studies programs at the UAW Family Education Center in Black Lake, Michigan, arguments flared over whether labor studies was the same as or included "occupational education" and "vocational training." [4]

In the most comprehensive survey of community college labor studies programs, 70 out of the 95 programs that said they were teaching "labor studies" were, according to William Abbott, the author of the survey report, "apparently management oriented." One college that claimed a "labor studies" program also said that it used supervision instructors to teach classes. The labor education office of the American Association of Community and Junior Colleges, which Abbott directed, tried to discourage casual use of the term. [5]

This was not a problem confined to the community college. Would the champions of "labor studies" welcome a program like Ohio State's graduate degree in labor and human resources (the euphemism for manpower) into the fold, or would they treat it like an alien enterprise?

Labor Studies on the Campus

The college campus in the 1970s represented fertile ground for the burgeoning of labor studies. The dominance of behaviorism and the decline of historical interpretation in the social sciences were pushing the study of labor out of the curriculum. Economics departments with a concentration of institutionally trained labor economists could once be counted on to generate interest in a wide range of labor topics. John R. Commons and his followers at Wisconsin and Harry Millis at University of Chicago did not confine themselves to economics: They were equally intrigued with labor history and social legislation.[6] The ascendancy of econometrics and neoclassical theory has gone hand in hand with the demise of the concerns of institutional economics.

In industrial relations, where the study of collective bargaining once had primacy, new areas, notably manpower and organizational behavior, were competing with it for influence.[7] As more faculty members with more academic interests were appointed, the industrial relations programs began to lose the direct connection to everyday labor issues they had had when under the sway of arbitrators and other practitioners. The labor arena, the industrial relations scholar Thomas Kochan argued, is well suited for the testing of social-science theories:

> The collective bargaining area offers an ideal laboratory for the study of organizational behavior concepts such as conflict and conflict resolution, bargaining theory, power environment-structure relations, boundary spanning roles, and the evaluation of the effectiveness of social systems. . . . Those interested in conceptualizing organizations as political systems composed of shifting coalitions and interest groups can benefit richly from the rich descriptive research that already exists in collective bargaining.[8]

DRAWING THE BOUNDARIES

The most elaborate attempt to define the contours of labor studies was done by three veteran labor educators, Herbert Levine, director of the Rutgers labor program, Helmut Golatz, director of the Penn State program, and John Mac-Kenzie, in their review of the master's in labor studies at the University of Massachusetts. The university established this degree, the first in the field, in 1965. The Labor Studies Center has used their statement (which has been widely circulated among university labor educators) several times in interpreting labor studies to administrators in our university. Systematically, this definition of labor studies takes up the challenge from industrial relations that we encountered in our clashes with the business school. It is worth quoting at length:

> It [labor studies] is a concept which is relatively new in the university setting. On the one hand, it acknowledges insights into the labor field which have recently emerged from several decades of university-union cooperation in labor education. On the other, it expresses an academic need to study labor affairs apart from the traditional framework of industrial relations.
>
> According to this concept, Labor Studies is the academic examination of problems which confront people in the pursuit of their need for rewarding employment. It is not the study of problems which face administrators in the management of people in their public and private enterprises. Thus Labor Studies is not Business Administration, or Public Administration, or Administrative Science; it does not pose the same set of questions. . . .
>
> Thus a comprehensive Labor Studies program takes as its focus the various organizations of workers and the internal and external relations of their unions to other societal institutions in the United States and around the world.[9]

The perspective of industrial relations, this definition insists, is too confining to encompass the wide-ranging activities of unions. Industrial relations focuses only on the union's dealings with management. These activities, the authors argue, are only one dimension of unions; in addition, they carry on political action, lobbying, community service programs, educational projects, and manpower training, to name a few of their functions. Labor studies examines the union as an organization and social institution in its own right, while industrial relations studies it only as an object of management's strategy for control. Many labor educators share the discomfort of these authors with the dependent position of the union in the industrial relations scheme. Russell Allen, deputy director of the George Meany Center for Labor Studies, proposes that the union, in the eyes of industrial relations, is merely an "appendage of management."[10]

Courses that illuminate "the trade union and its internal and external functions," the statement's framers suggest, in the tradition of the Wisconsin school, could be the heart of a labor studies curriculum. These core courses would sharpen the focus of the University of Massachusetts program, which functioned to a large degree as a broker for the labor offerings of other departments.[11] Moreover, leaders of the field feel that labor studies courses should be taught by faculty loyal to the institution being studied. The hallmark of labor studies, Herbert Levine contends, is its assiduous attention to its clients. Industrial relations, in his view, is "subject oriented" in its single-minded devotion to academic study.[12]

In the absence of strong social commitments from the faculty, the career aspirations of students will go undisturbed. Labor educators continue to be struck by how few of the graduates of industrial relations programs take positions in the labor movement. A 1976 survey of their alumni by Cornell's School of Industrial and Labor Relations showed that only 3 percent held positions with trade unions, whereas 46 percent held management posts.[13] Writing in a symposium on the ILR School, Harold Newman, a former faculty member and then Director of Conciliation of New York State's Public-Employee Relations Board, was disturbed about the aspirations of students: "I think the School may unconsciously foster the notion that it is a kind of preparatory school for law school."[14]

The shapers of this new field, however, have yet to convince even all their friends that it is as unique as they insist. In the aftermath of one of the inevitable discussions at a UCLEA conference on defining labor studies, one veteran labor educator said that he couldn't understand what all the fussing was about. What difference was there, he asked, between labor studies and industrial relations? His confusion was natural given the resemblance between some of the courses offered in labor studies programs and those given in industrial relations schools. An ambitious field, labor studies embraced such traditional industrial relations subjects as labor law, arbitration, collective bargaining, and labor economics while extending its reach to areas ignored by industrial relations. The result has been that a program can occupy the gray area between the two fields. The West Virginia Institute of Technology, a member of the UCLEA, offers a degree in labor studies and industrial relations.

Industrial Relations: A Discipline?

Industrial relations, the discipline to which the exponents of labor studies were reacting, was also a relative newcomer on the college campus. It, too, struggled to win academic standing, to achieve more than interdisciplinary status. As John Dunlop, one of the most prominent architects of the field in the post–World War II period, argued in 1947, a strong degree program in industrial relations awaited the building of a knowledge base for the discipline:

> Although industrial relations aspires to be a discipline, and even though there exist separate professional societies, industrial relations has lacked any central analytical content. It has been a crossroads where a number of disciplines have met—history, economics, government, sociology, psychology, and law.[15]

To do this, industrial relations had to break its ties to economics. In *Industrial Relations Systems*, Dunlop's attempt to

fashion a theoretical foundation for the discipline, he set off
the boundaries of the two fields:

> An industrial relations system is not a subsidiary part of an
> economic system but is rather a separate and distinctive sub-
> system of the society, on the same plane as an economic system.
> Thus, the theoretical tools designed to explain the economic
> system are not likely to be entirely suitable to another different
> analytical subsystem of society.[16]

The core of industrial relations, Dunlop said, was a study
of the rules that shaped the relationship among management,
government, and the "hierarchy of workers." The unraveling
of industrial relations in the 1960s and the assertion of
independence by areas once woven together, such as labor law
and organizational behavior, intensified the search for unify-
ing elements in the field.[17] Some scholars, notably Columbia
economist Neil Chamberlain, however, claimed that industrial relations lacked the characteristics of a discipline:

> Our field sprawls and the territory we have staked out takes in a
> polyglot lot of inhabitants with diffuse and often separate inter-
> ests. . . . If one stops to consider what constitutes the bond of
> association between those who inhabit our professional territory,
> he is driven back on the thin line of defense that it includes all
> those whose interests are touched by labor. . . . In each of its
> many contexts and conceptual forms, "labor" may be an instru-
> ment for organizing knowledge, but as a single enveloping interest
> it is without content and no more useful in organizing knowledge
> than would be, for example, the effort to relate the study of
> money in whatever context it is found.[18]

Students interested in industrial relations, he felt, would be
better off choosing a traditional discipline.

THE BATTLE FOR RECOGNITION

The drafters of the University of Massachusetts statement on
labor studies had more than a theoretical interest in their

work. All of the feverish formulations of the field over the last decade have been of tactical importance: They have been used as platforms in the contest for university recognition. The leaders of the labor studies movement have learned that their programs would be fragile without a firm academic base.

The absence of an industrial relations program at Penn State created a favorable climate for constructing a labor studies program. A Department of Labor Education, created in 1955, housed both the labor extension program and an undergraduate major in labor-management relations. As the labor courses in other departments dropped off and the Department of Labor Education sharpened its own focus, Helmut Golatz, the department head, moved the emphasis of the curriculum away from labor relations. "Labor studies," not "labor-management relations," became the underpinning of the course of study, and the department was so renamed:

> the Department of Labor Education has discovered that its own perspective was too limiting . . . labor is no longer perceived as one aspect of industrial relations; instead industrial relations is viewed as one of several arenas on which the labor presence impinges.[19]

Herbert Levine, director of the Rutgers program, battled the supporters of industrial relations on the campus as he tried to build a master's degree in labor studies. Pushed by the research unit of the Institute of Management and Labor Relations and supported by the top academic administrators at Rutgers, the proposal for a master's in industrial relations sailed through the university approval committees. The School of Business interestingly enough showed little enthusiasm for the proposal and gave it no active support. The proponents of the industrial relations degree assumed that it encompassed the study of labor, and that consequently there was no need for a separate master's in labor studies.[20]

Without the intervention of Joel Jacobson, a UAW official who was a member of the Rutgers Board of Governors and a strong ally of the Rutgers labor program, the proposal for the master's in labor studies would not have reached the Board at the same time as did the one for industrial relations.[21] Even after both degrees were approved (both began programs in 1974), the industrial relations faculty was still bent on scuttling the labor studies degree. The faculty's position was strengthened by the report of an outside review committee on the industrial relations and labor studies programs, the majority of whose members urged that the two be merged. The reviewers envisioned a core curriculum uniting the combined program. The courses they suggested for possible inclusion in the core were such industrial relations staples as Research Methods and Statistics, Personnel Management, and Manpower Economics, coupled with labor studies offerings such as Union History and Administration, Collective Bargaining, and Labor Law.[22] The business school's proposals for a joint degree with our program had similar shades to it.

The Rutgers labor program criticized the review committee's "unrealistic recommendation—to combine administratively and budgetarily programs in labor studies and industrial relations which are substantively different in curriculum and clientele support." Its attack on this proposal concluded:

> It is a historical fact that American unions and most other unions in the world have supported labor education and labor studies programs but have made very little use of university industrial relations programs. It appears that not all members of the committee were sufficiently aware of this fact. Those who took a minority position against combination, wisely refraining from the double folly of putting new wine (two kinds) into old wine-skins.[23]

DEPARTMENTAL STATUS

The strategy for academic independence required that labor studies have full departmental status. It was here that faculty would receive appointments and train its successors. Without this protection labor studies programs could easily become ephemeral organizations subject to all the pressures and incentives of the faculty's parent departments.

The director and associate director of the University of Massachusetts program had appointments not in labor studies but in political science and management, respectively, a situation that worried the review committee examining it:

> The current two faculty members assigned to the Labor Center suffer a number of professional and personal handicaps which it appears possible to alleviate by administrative action. . . . It seems unfair for faculty working in Labor Studies to be assessed and rewarded by criteria of political science and management. Since the Director of the program has won institutional and personal recognition on the national scene, it would appear that he would have long since achieved the rank of full professor if he had been assessed in relation to criteria for labor educators.[24]

This recognition, as the experience of American studies demonstrates, is not easily won. The founders of that field, which arose because of the low status given to the study of American culture in English and history departments, stepped gingerly around these powerful disciplines in its early years. Many faculty in the 1940s and 1950s did not push for appointments in American studies but instead were hired by English and history departments. The leadership of the American Studies Association reflected the preeminence of other disciplines. The association elected its first American studies Ph.D. in 1970–71, nineteen years after it was founded.[25]

Programs began as a vehicle for offerings with an American slant from other departments. In 1958 more than half of the graduate programs did not teach a single American studies course. By the 1970s American studies had markedly improved its position. The signs of its success were the growth of independent departments and faculty appointments in the field.[26]

Hiring Standards for Labor Studies Faculty

To attain the prize of academic standing, labor studies would have to accommodate the demand that it adhere to university standards, particularly those involving criteria for faculty. When the Labor Studies Center ran a largely extension operation, questions of credentials could be more easily skirted. We now had to reconcile our preference for hiring some faculty with trade union and labor education experience, but without the formal academic qualifications with the college's standards for hiring. Recruiting qualified Ph.D.'s for our teaching posts would not be easy in a field where the master's was more often the norm. Those few labor educators who have received doctorates have done their work in areas other than labor studies—in education, sociology, economics, even English literature. Faced with this dilemma, MacKenzie worked out an informal understanding with Dr. John Jenkins, then dean of the School of Education, that he would hire younger candidates with Ph.D.'s while making exceptions for older, more experienced trade unionists with a strong leadership background.

Our assumptions about the merits of practical experience for college faculty were not at all self-evident to the members of the committees before whom we appeared. After hearing MacKenzie describe Arthur Kane, then education director of AFGE and part-time teacher for the center, as an ideal candidate for full professor, one professor on the Academic Policy Committee expressed complete bewilderment. A full professor himself, he wondered how we could contemplate conferring such a rank on an individual who only had an undergraduate degree.[27]

The issue of the proper credentials for labor program staff was not unique to our program. The Graduate School faculty committee reviewing the proposal for the Master's in labor studies submitted by the Rutgers labor program chided it for the insufficient number of advanced degrees among their projected faculty. Teachers in the industrial relations program objected to plans for former trade unionists without undergraduate degrees to be teaching graduate courses. In order to allay the fears of the review committee and still maintain the teachers in the program the committee was challenging, Herbert Levine added several well-credentialed professors from social-science departments to his faculty roster.[28] These teachers have given the program valuable support, but that they had to be added at all underscores the pressures that university labor programs are bound to be under.

In anticipation of similar objections from our faculty and administration, our staff decided tht we needed a set of criteria to equate work experience with the degree and teaching experience requirements for the various academic ranks. Since the Board of Higher Education permitted departments to do just this, we drafted a statement, "Equivalency Criteria for Employment and Promotion of Faculty Members in Lieu of Academic Degree and Teaching Experience."[29] MacKenzie had helped us to establish such a position in his request to the president for promotion from associate to full professor. His long teaching and administrative experience, together with his master's degree, the terminal degree in the field, he argued, more than justified this promotion. We stated our rationale for seeking an exception to the hiring standards in our document:

> Although we will make every effort to recruit Ph.D.s in related disciplines, it will be necessary to hire experienced labor educators whose professional and executive capability and experience outweigh their lack of formal credentials. We wish to employ a faculty that combines a unique blend of academic, trade union, and government experience. Washington has a wealth of talent in the field of labor studies who will add stature to our program. We will draw on adjunct instructors from labor organizations, government agencies, other UDC departments and other universities to teach in their particular areas of expertise. However, we also

need the mechanism to employ experienced labor studies professionals within the full-time faculty structure.[30]

We proposed the number of years of labor experience that could be substituted for degrees (a minimum of six years for the master's; a minimum of eight years for the doctorate) and for years of formal teaching. Experience that could cancel out the colleges' requirements would have to be of an exemplary kind:

> Experience qualifications are defined as those activities demonstrating intensive and extensive leadership positions in union/labor rules exemplified by their holding the offices in line and staff positions and/or positions of responsibility within union or labor organizational structures.[31]

The university has yet to approve our proposal.

THE OBSTACLES TO ACADEMIC STANDING

The prospect of a rival degree-granting field arouses natural fears and jealousies among the programs whose boundaries it crosscuts. The institutionalist defense of labor studies is certan to stiffen the natural resistance of the academy's elders to interlopers. Many are bound to question how a field can found its uniqueness not on the basis of a distinctive approach to knowledge but merely on its total concentration on the trade union. Promoters of the discipline could disarm their competitors more effectively by widening the compass of labor studies to cover the experience of work in the United States and abroad. By adopting this theme, labor studies would be staking out an area in which the traditional social sciences are weakest.

People in the field would do well to emulate the "new labor historians" in the United States, who have covered a wider terrain than that of the trade union. This group of historians —Herbert Gutman, Alan Dawley, David Brody, and others —did not want to reduce the study of workers to an account of their economic organizations. To do so, they felt, would render invisible all but the modest percentage of laboring people the trade unions have enrolled. An interpretation fixed on the union also slights the other varied settings—community, family, ethnic group, work place—in which organized and unorganized workers have expressed themselves. This new approach to labor history has not written off the trade union; rather, it has made it a critical element on a broader social canvas.[32]

Some of the architects of labor studies have tried to redefine the field along these lines. With some notable exceptions, labor studies programs have not been influenced by the formulation that Richard Dwyer, Miles Galvin, and Simeon Larson, all teaching at Rutgers at the time, offered in a fall 1977 article in *Labor Studies Journal:*

> Labor studies sets for itself the task of examining the nature of work, the individual's relationship to work, the organizations workers form to protect their interests, and those institutions and non-work phenomena that are affected by, and, in turn, affect the work process and the workers.[33]

Even with a sharply defined intellectual core, labor studies will continue to depend to a large degree on the tools, perspective, and knowledge developed by other longer-standing disciplines, such as political science, sociology, and history. The power of law and economics, whose graduates are still the most sought after of union specialists, is still formidable. To that extent, like American studies and urban studies, labor studies will have to come to some rapprochement with its competitors.

The desire of the labor studies program to be in but not of the university is also bound to irritate some professors. Labor studies programs are seeking degree-granting authority, but at the same time they are asking for exceptions to the rules under which other departments are governed. The arbiters of the infant discipline's fate are certain to demand that it modify, if not eliminate, this paradoxical stance.

Notes

1. Remarks of Dale Brickner, director, Labor Program Service, and then president of the University College Labor Education Association, to the Joint Conference on Labor Education, Walter and May Reuther UAW Family Education Center, November 15, 1976.

2. Dorothy Ross, "The Development of the Social Sciences," in Alexandra Oleson and John Voss (eds.), *The Organization of Knowledge in Modern America 1860–1920* (Baltimore: Johns Hopkins University Press, 1979).

3. "Proposal for a Master's Degree in Labor Studies," submitted by Labor Studies Center, School of Education, Federal City College, 1976 (revised 1977), p. 1.

4. The reference is to the Joint Conference on Labor Education, Walter and May Reuther UAW Family Education Center, November 14–17, 1976, cosponsored by the University and College Labor Education Association, the American Association of Community and Junior Colleges, the UAW, and the AFL-CIO.

5. William Abbott, "College/Labor Union Cooperation," reprinted in *Community and Junior College Journal* (April 1977): 3.

6. George Strauss and Peter Feuille, "Industrial Relations Research: A Critical Analysis," *Industrial Relations* 17, no. 3 (October 1978): 261.

7. Ibid., pp. 267–68, 275.

8. Quoted in ibid., p. 271.

9. "Visitation Committee Report M.S. in Labor Studies," November 1976, pp. 1–2.

10. Interview with Russell Allen, Silver Spring, Maryland, June 3, 1980.

11. "Visitation Committee Report," p. 6.

12. Interview with Dr. Herbert Levine, Bangor, Maine, April 7, 1977.

13. "The School: Education in the Crossroads," *Industrial and Labor Relations Report* 13, no. 1 (Fall 1976): 24.

14. Ibid., p. 11.

15. John T. Dunlop, *Industrial Relations Systems* (New York: Henry Holt and Company, 1958), p. 6.

16. Ibid., p. 5.

17. Strauss and Feuille, "Industrial Relations Research," pp. 266–67.

18. Quoted in Milton Derber, "Divergent Tendencies in Industrial Relations Research," *Industrial and Labor Relations Review* 17, no. 4 (July 1964): 600.

19. "Annual Report of Activities September 1, 1975–August 31, 1976," Department of Labor Studies, Penn State University, p. 2.

20. Interview with Dr. Herbert Levine, Bangor; interview with Dr. Herbert Levine, Washington, D.C., July 28, 1977.

21. Interview with Dr. Herbert Levine, Washington.

22. "Rutgers University Master of Arts in Industrial Relations Degree," prepared by Richard V. Miller and David B. Lipsky, n.d., p. 2.

23. *Comments on the Summary Report and Recommendations and Other Reports of the Education Committee for Rutgers University I.M.L.R. and Graduate and Undergraduate Degree Programs for Industrial Relations and Labor Studies*, n.d., p. 3.

24. "Visitation Committee Report," p. 11.

25. Leo Marx, "Thoughts on the Origin and Character of the American Studies Movement," *American Studies Quarterly* 31, no. 3 (Bibliography Issue, 1979): 398–99; Gene Wise, " 'Paradigm Dramas' in American Studies: A Cultural and Institutional History of the Movement," *American Studies Quarterly* 31, no. 3 (Bibliography Issue, 1979): 328–29.

26. Wise, "Paradigm Dramas," p. 329.

27. Notes on Academic Policy Committee meeting, September 2, 1976.

28. Interview with Dr. Herbert Levine, Bangor.

29. Labor Studies Center University of the District of Columbia, "Equivalency Criteria for Employment and Promotion of Faculty Members in Lieu of Academic Degree and Teaching Experience," May 1, 1977.

30. Ibid., p. 2.

31. Ibid., p. 3.

32. See David Brody, "The Old Labor History and the New: In Search of an American Working Class," *Labor History* 20, no. 1 (Winter 1979): 111–26; Ronald L. Filippelli, "The Uses of History in the Education of Workers," *Labor Studies Journal* 5, no. 1 (Spring 1980): 3–12.

33. Richard E. Dwyer, Miles E. Galvin, and Simeon Larson, "Labor Studies: In Quest of Industrial Justice," *Labor Studies Journal* 2, no. 2 (Fall 1977): 125.

4

Unions and Universities: A Change in the Balance of Power

The rise of the labor studies programs threatens to change the historic ties that have developed between unions and universities by increasing the power of independent faculty. A wariness of higher education led unions to seek only the most carefully delimited relationship with universities. It was a relationship that gave the union the maximum in bargaining power.

A good part of this distrust of universities derived from seeing them as the captives of business interests. College conjured up an image of a hidebound institution run by a conservative board of trustees with little sympathy for the plight of workers. James Maurer, president of the Pennsylvania Federation of Labor during the 1920s, pilloried the public school and the universities for their reactionary sentiments. His statement reflects a mood that still lingers today:

> The college-bred labour-haters who have assumed the "patriotic" duty of helping to break railroad and street car strikes are

"products" that American colleges like to boast of. . . . The workingmen's children return from school with accounts of indictments of the labor movement made by their teachers . . . children have been led to feel that their own teachers, as active unionists, have been made the dupes of treasonable conspirators. . . . Workingmen have also observed the snobbishness of the average school teacher. If she shows any sympathy for workingmen and their families it is the condescending sympathy that is worse than contempt. Her male colleagues up in the high school . . . are even worse snobs than she for they are trying to hobnob with members of the chambers of commerce, rotary clubs, and similar organizations.[1]

The first steps in the forging of a relationship between the unions and universities were tentative, halting ones. Union hesitancy showed up in refusals by some organizations to register the names of members attending courses and in occasional demands that only the union should issue the certificate awarded at the completion of a university program. University interference resulted in limitations or outright vetoes on controversial courses in such areas as organizing, strike strategy, and labor political action.[2]

Unions were groping for a partnership that would meld two institutions with sharply contrasting styles. In one of the earliest reports on university labor programs, *Labor Education in Universities*, published in 1946, the time of the flowering of these ventures, Caroline Ware pointed to the differences keeping them apart:

It is difficult for labor people to understand the loose organization of a university and its lack of centralized direction, the autonomy of departments, the independence of individual faculty members, the devotion to the scientific method, and the fact that a university can harbor and give scope to people of widely different views. Workers are used to the disciplined organization of industry under which they work and to their unions organized for common action under the more or less tight leadership of their top officials.[3]

Unions found that training cosponsored with a university labor center met their institutional needs and was the most comfortable arrangement. Extension programs were a vehicle in which unions felt they could exercise maximum leverage with minimum interference from the university. Since short courses offered without credit were peripheral to the main activities of the universities, the customary controls clamped upon classes leading to a degree would not be imposed on them.

Their connection with the university would be through a separate unit with an exclusively labor constituency. Training would be given at their request and would reflect the priorities they insisted on in planning sessions with labor center representatives. Students would be recruited through the union, and the union would decide which candidates to finance.

Similarly, farm bureaus used the cooperative extension service as their entree to the landgrant universities. The farm bureau leadership, Robert Wiebe argues, developed strong ties to the county agents who ran programs for these powerful agricultural organizations.[4]

University and union educators worked out a rationale for the relationship between their respective institutions at a conference at Rutgers University on April 30, 1962. The statement they produced was an attempt to harmonize what might otherwise have been antagonistic objectives:

> Universities can and should render genuine educational services to organized labor groups, just as they have been rendering services for years to business, farmers and other functional groups in our society. . . . Further, it requires of universities an acceptance of the principles and methods of workers education and its institutional channels within the unions. And it requires of unions a recognition of the need of universities to maintain objectivity, intellectual integrity and standards of teaching.[5]

The cornerstone of the bond between union and university

was to be the labor advisory committee, a committee made up of university representatives, key union officers in the state, and leaders from national unions. The Rutgers statement envisioned the committee as the primary instrument for giving direction to and promoting university labor institutes.[6] One survey of advisory committees at twenty eight universities showed that they almost always included state federation or local centralbody officers.[7]

To protect their stake in the university, unions have thrown their political weight behind the labor centers. They have lobbied adeptly to increase funding for these programs and to protect them from cutbacks. At times, by wielding political clout, union allies have secured an independent subsidy for the labor institute, a fund separate from general extension. At a conference one highranking state federation official spoke of the debts incurred by legislators that labor had worked for. They should repay these debts, he said, by supporting university programs for trade unionists. "Payday," he argued, had arrived.

Labor educators quickly learn to cultivate the contacts in the legislatures provided by their ties with trade unions. The Rutgers labor program, which has developed this knack almost to perfection, mobilized legislators behind a bill to appropriate funds for its center, a bill separate from the general university budget. When the president of the university learned of this, he forced the withdrawal of the bill. But the influence the program displayed enabled its director, Herbert Levine, to extract future commitments from the top university officer.

The lobbying ability of the unions can be put to work in behalf of the entire state university budget, not just that of the labor program. The promise of such powerful backing can overcome hesitations university administrators might otherwise feel about a labor program. At one state university, talks about establishing an institute were at a standstill until the president mentioned to the state federation president the difficulties his budget was having in the legislature. The union officer immediately offered his assistance.

A canny president can capitalize on the lines to the union hierarchy that a labor center provides in developing and expanding the services of a large state university. The late Mason Gross, when president of Rutgers University, would bring in Joel Jacobson, a top Auto Workers official on the Board of Trustees, on many of his major tactical decisions.[8]

The principles of cooperation of the Rutgers statement have often been difficult to realize, and tensions between the two parties have simmered just below the surface. Union representatives sitting on labor advisory committees have often resented them for being pro forma institutions, ritual exercises used by the university educators to win assent to decisions already made. At the annual AFL-CIO Education Conference in 1976, a meeting of union and university labor educators, Lawrence Scott, an international representative of the Machinists, voiced a common complaint:

> I think many of them tend to become confirmation committees. The university education staff gets up and tells about all the wonderful things they have done the last year and then the union endorses and everyone goes to lunch. Those meetings are a waste.[9]

In return for their political support and sponsorship of programs, labor leaders expect a correspondingly strong voice in determining what will be taught in class. Mistrust increases when labor leaders detect opposition to union policies being sparked in university programs. William Marshall, president of the Michigan State AFL-CIO, stated emphatically what he expects out of his state's labor centers:

> Hardly a single year goes by that we aren't called upon by the universities to go to bat for them in the legislative halls in Lansing to help them secure an adequate budget for the overall programs of the universities. . . . We have had to fight like tigers to maintain these programs. So, to that extent, I believe we are

partners in these programs and I disagree we should not have anything to say about what they teach. . . . If I am going to lend the name of the AFL-CIO to a labor education program, if I am going to permit members of my staff to participate in that program and if I am going to make a mailing, which we do to all the affiliates and local unions, if I am going to use our computer to do that at a cost to the AFL-CIO, then I think we have a right at least to sit down and discuss what they are going to teach.[10]

Education directors of national unions holding institutes at universities expect instructors to hew closely to union policies. Ted Valliere, former education director of the American Postal Workers Union, recounted times when he had been stung by university challenges to strongly held positions of his organization:

We have had problems with universities that get involved in the policy of our union. We had some very definite problems when we first went into the Postal Reorganization Act in 1971 and universities tried to interpret our contract to the membership. They brought in lawyers, mind you, to interpret the contract of the American Postal Workers Union. It created all kinds of problems. We have had the same problems with grievances that George [George Butsika, education director of the United Steelworkers of America] has had. "Give them a fair shot, send them all the way up." Over the duration of our last contract we had 15,000 grievances. Currently 2,000 are pending arbitration. We do have some problems in that area with universities when they promote moving grievances to arbitration.[11]

University labor educators learn to step deftly to avoid being drawn into decisions on union policy. I had to retreat gracefully when one member of my collective bargaining class from the St. Elizabeth's local asked me to write up sample contract clauses.

On their side, university centers frequently feel slighted by the limited role they are allowed to play in union programs on their campuses, particularly the one-week summer schools organized by national unions. Labor institutes are miffed when their universities are chosen for negative reasons—for example, because their facilities are more desirable than a hotel's. Universities would like to be regarded as more than hotels with "atmosphere," an image that Charles Crown's (education director of the Machinists) rationale for campus-based summer schools evokes:

> Most of our leadership and staff training schools are a week long and most of these are done in university facilities. It is much better to go into a university and use its facilities, eat together, study together and remain on campus for a week and to create an educational atmosphere than to have a conference atmosphere at a hotel or convention site. [12]

Wariness of university teachers for their lack of rapport with workers and tendency to stray into matters of union policy has led some national unions to staff summer schools largely with their own officials. George Butsika former education director of the Steelworkers, voiced such misgivings:

> Universities can help, but I don't think we should leave the responsibility solely to the universities to staff our programs. They do not understand the problems that arise day to day in the mills or mines. These are areas that only a person who deals with these problems everyday can understand and can determine the type of teaching which is necessary. It is the international union that sets policy that can best teach these courses. Only the union staff knows the policy of the international. [13]

Other unions, particularly those for which the education department functions as a vigorous arm of union policy such as in the Amalgamated Clothing and Textile Workers Union, tend to avoid universities altogether.

Friction between unions and universities springs to a large degree from the decentralized structure of labor education and the labor movement itself. Unions and universities frequently operate independently of each other and often vie for the same turf. Colleges and universities have enlarged their role considerably so that they do a majority of the union training. [14] Since most of their work is done with local unions in their jurisdictions, they are bound to brush shoulders with the locals' parent unions. National education directors are sometimes irked when universities develop these relationships without consulting them.

Neither unions nor universities receive any central direction from the AFL-CIO's Education Department in carrying out their programs. The AFL-CIO performs the role of umpire in the educational arena and more typically operates on a passive basis, in response to requests from member unions. Directors of university labor programs sometimes can sway a national union more effectively than can the federation's Education Department.

The picture of labor education as a "fragmented" enterprise that Lawrence Rogin and Marjorie Rachlin drew in 1968 still rings true:

> In the United States there is no national, comprehensive system of labor education. Each institution develops its own program as it sees fit. This is true for the individual unions as well as the other organizations that sponsor labor education. Labor education is therefore a fragmented field, each union and each university center determining how much it will do and developing its own priorities, its own methods of operations, its own materials, and its own program identity.[15]

Credit Programs and Union Power

Rancorous as the conflicts between universities and unions have been, they have at least been fought within a framework in which the labor organization could exercise leverage or at least had a semblance of control. What worries organized labor, even while it is drawn to accept the trend toward degree programs, is that it will lose its strong voice as the pressure for credentialing intensifies. The advent of credit, it is feared, will tilt the balance of power to the advantage of independent faculty, who are less likely to heed the advice of trade unionists. The cries from the unions that faculty should have "trade union experience," or better yet be union officials, and that the only road to leadership is through experience are rooted in this fear of losing control. Other voices in labor education circles urge the universities to stick to their traditional role of bread-and-butter courses and union leadership training.

Occasionally, the suspicion is expressed that the spiraling labor studies courses are not a response to worker demands, but a cynical attempt by colleges to expand their markets. One labor leader at a conference I attended assailed the community colleges for being interested solely in signing up "bodies." There are echoes here of the sourness with which many farmers greeted the creation of land-grant universities. The growth of these institutions got its momentum more from the promotion of rural modernizers, such as editors of agricultural journals and gentlemen farmers, than from the urgings of ordinary agrarians. The comments of the Wisconsin Grange that "Ecclesiastics should teach ecclesiastics, lawyers teach lawyers, mechanics teach mechanics, and farmers teach farmers" have their counterparts in the rhetoric about university labor education.[16]

There are definite signs in the expansion of academic-based programs to warrant the fears of trade unionists and of veteran labor educators. Degree programs represent a sharp departure in style from labor education as it has been traditionally understood. If credit courses are pushed too uncritically, there is a danger that university labor education will disassociate itself even further from its historical roots. If they do not want to abandon their central mission of extension and local service, labor educators should be alert to the pitfalls that could ensnare them in pursuit of this course.

As labor centers concentrate their energies less at the margins of the academy, unions will lose their central advisory roles. The focus of degree programs on admitting individual students according to university criteria means that the influence of institutional channels and political norms will be substantially diminished. The job of recruitment and the financing of students, which fall heavily on the union in an extension program, will revert more to the hands of faculty, university officials, and the degree candidates themselves.

Unions will have less influence over the kinds of classes to be taught as curriculum decisions are placed in the hands of faculty and university approval bodies. The ease with which an individual union could request a course or the members of an advisory committee make its pleasures known in a labor extension service will be difficult, if not impossible, to duplicate in a degree program.

The change in power relationships will restrict the ability of unions to enforce their claims to a say in subject matter that bears on union policy. The faculty member's academic freedom, a concept many trade unions are uncomfortable with, makes him the arbiter of course content.

CREDIT VERSUS EXTENSION PROGRAMS:
THE DIFFERENCE IN STYLE

Credit programs have a markedly different flavor than extension short courses and conferences. The weakening of advisory committees and the joint planning process make the curriculum less organic. It can easily become an array of courses worked out by the faculty in relative isolation and then dispensed to the students.

Teaching simultaneously in an extension class and in credit courses was a jarring experience for me. The short bargaining course I taught for the St. Elizabeth's local was done at its request in response to a specific need: The local needed skills in order to renegotiate its agreement. As one of the members observed, the class was attractive because it was not chosen from a "list." Many of the topics we focused on were determined in discussions between myself and the local leadership. An additional drawing card was its location at the union hall, nor far from the hospital.

In contrast, the classes in labor history and labor education I was teaching on the graduate level, however exciting to me, seemed remote from the practical situations of my students. I rarely felt that the students were gaining tools that they could immediately put to use. The unease I felt reflected the difference between the origins of the two classes—one asked for and taken at considerable sacrifice without credit, the other attended because the course description intrigued students and met their course requirements.

The style of labor extension, its ad hoc, how-to-do-it manner, contrasts with the more theoretical, deductive cast of labor studies. At its best, it is this action orientation that links labor education to what is distinctive in the workers' education tradition. Hilda Smith, director of the Bryn Mawr School for Women Workers and the WPA Workers Education program, nicely sums up the approach of workers education:

> It has sometimes been said that in workers' education the teachers do not ask the student, "What do you want to study?" but "What do you want to do, and how can we help you do it?" In the difference between these two questions lies the difference between the usual academic class and one in workers' education. . . .
>
> But what may actually happen as the result of a workers' class is in direct human terms; individuals and groups trying to do something for their families, their organizations, their home towns; and doing it a little more effectively, perhaps, because they have studied, debated, and acted upon these matters together. . . .
>
> A group of unemployed workers, living in shacks, begin to study local housing laws, and as a result succeed in interesting the mayor and the town council in a new housing project. . . . A laundry worker, who through her class has become aware of sanitary standards, reports bad conditions in her laundry to the local health department, at the risk of losing her own job.[17]

A short course will try to equip students with techniques for handling grievances, while a credit class will examine a steward's job in the overall framework of labor relations. Functional training, however, is not simply laid on unsuspecting trade unionists, as some critics of labor education's pragmatism have charged; often it develops from the actual preference of workers. As much as our staff would have liked to sign up union members for labor history classes, workers voted with their feet for courses in public speaking and steward's training.

William Abbott, when he was education director of the United Rubber Workers, tried to interest members in broader social issues, but his efforts often floundered because of the appeal of more tangible subjects. He established an experimental summer program with the University of Akron, in which the union paid for members to take classes from an offering evenly divided between liberal arts and practical courses. Interest was minimal in such fields as world affairs, political science, economics, and sociology. The most popular subjects were public speaking, basic English, and remedial writing. Abbott found that the only way he could inject social content into his programs was to have a "captive audience" at summer schools. There he could require members to attend courses in labor history and contemporary issues.

There is a danger that credit instruction in labor studies will take its cue less from the student's immediate concerns, the hallmark of workers' education, and more from the internal logic of the discipline. This would turn labor education into a "subject" rather than a "client"-oriented field, to use Herbert Levine's distinction between labor education and industrial relations.

Materials production, once a trademark of labor education and now a lackluster enterprise, risks further decline under a regime of credit. Instructors are more likely to use standard texts or to write them than to improvise materials to meet constantly changing demands from worker-students.

The bonds between labor education and adult education, once tight and now tenuous, are bound to weaken more as the style of university programs becomes more formalized. Eduard Lindeman, Horace Kallen, George Counts, and others were deeply interested in the early development of workers' education, and their progressive education outlook left its imprint on these programs.

As the star of credit in labor programs rises, will the standing of their extension service fall? The natural dynamic of the academy is to elevate degree instruction and to relegate noncredit teaching to a lower status. The reward structure of the university—the incentives that determine faculty rank, promotion, and standing among one's colleagues—reflects a pecking order in which academic teaching and research stand at the pinnacle and mundane local service rates very poorly.

Labor centers will have to struggle mightily to resist a kind of "Gresham's Law," to use the writer Ronald Gross's image, in which credit crowds out work of lesser currency. Within one labor center there is a risk that resources such as funding and staff will be diverted to academic programs and that its extension wing will shrink in importance. Recognition in the university may go to campus-based faculty, and instructors in the field, the circuit-riders to the local unions, may remain anonymous.

At Cornell's School of Industrial and Labor Relations, the resident faculty has enjoyed greater status than teachers in the extension service. Traditional academics have the vote at faculty meetings, while the majority of extension teachers do not. Only those extension teachers who meet the requirements established by the academic departments are given professorial rank. The effort made in the school's early days to have professors teach in both the extension and resident division was thwarted because of the academic faculty's lack of enthusiasm.[18]

Herbert Levine, director of the Rutgers labor program, worried about how easily the academic departments he had launched took on a life of their own, detached from the program's historic base, its extension service. Levine was concerned about the tendency of academic faculties to develop their own power bases at odds with the parent labor center.[19]

The Criteria for a Labor Studies Faculty

The extent to which status divisions are heightened hinges to a great extent on the character of the faculty chosen in the new degree programs and the tone it sets. If labor studies programs follow the example of other new professional degrees—social work, city planning, nursing—in insisting on academic training and credentials as the prime requirement for faculty, they are likely to find their new instructors unsympathetic to extension teaching.[20] The status pressures placed on a new discipline, coupled with the demands of university hiring standards, may lead labor studies programs to hire candidates with doctorates over those with practical experience but without these credentials.

Some such faculty may scorn service work for the more prestigious assignments of academic teaching, research, and publication. To use David Riesman's image, "cosmopolitans," who see their role in the context of a national academic community, are inclined to look down upon "locals," who may be carrying on outreach programs. Similarly, they may feel a strong impulse to reshape the labor program in the image of their own graduate school experiences.

University policies that rank academic teaching above extension in evaluating faculty are likely to reinforce the temptation of faculty to avoid noncredit work. In addition, the tendency of the academy to consume one's time with committee assignments, departmental duties, and other campus priorities diverts energies that might otherwise go into extension teaching.

Even if pressed to teach courses in the field, academically trained faculty may lack the knack for or at least not have

experience in relating to workers. Instead of organizing discussions around the concerns that trade unionists bring to
class, they may fall back on prearranged lectures. In 1946
Caroline Ware emphasized the difficulties she expected teachers in the first postwar university programs would have in
extablishing a rapport with workers:

> Universities have entered the field with faculties and administra-
> tors most of whose members have had little or no contact with
> labor, have shown little or no aptitude in dealing with workers in
> the classroom, and have little or no experience in the teaching
> methods which have been found to be effective in workers
> education in the past.[21]

The problem will be more severe with the rise of credentialing.

At Federal City few barriers existed between the extension
and credit units of our center. John MacKenzie encouraged
the kind of flexibility that enabled me to teach in both sides of
the program. I felt that the nourishment of grass-roots teaching made me more effective in an academic classroom. But the
college was still a fluid one, an institution in which our labor
center could maneuver around the formal criteria that did
exist. Would I be able to play such a freewheeling role when
we had a full-fledged degree program to administer and the
university had fully rationalized its standards for faculty
advancement? In addition, we were operating in a college
with only a small graduate school, an institution without the
strong departmental models to which our modest efforts
would be inevitably compared.

An imbalance of faculty trained in academic disciplines can
also create distortions in the teaching of a credit program. The
more leavening from practitioners, the less likelihood that the
research interests of faculty will be elevated above the necessi-
ties of career preparation. A sociologist, psychologist, or
economist may find it difficult to draw on his specialty to
illuminate the problems students will face as practitioners. If a

professor builds his course around the questions posed by his academic discipline, he may encourage students to abandon their immediate goals for the prospect of careers in teaching or research. Since the academic faculty is likely to hold a more prestigious degree (particularly if it is an academic rather than a professional credential) than the practitioners, its example will be that much more contagious.

The experience Nathan Glazer recounts of other new fields succumbing to the pressures of professionalization is not an especially heartening one:

> in schools of education, psychologists and sociologists, historians and philosophers, teach students who intend to become teachers, school principals and school superintendents; in schools of social work, various kinds of research workers teach students who intend to become social workers; and in schools of town planning, economists, political scientists, and sociologists teach students who intend to become practical town planners . . . in all schools, the route to higher professional standing lies in replacing the professionals and practitioners with the scholars and the research workers.[22]

The example of agriculture, an older, practical vocation that was incorporated into the university, underlines the snares of the academic path. Unlike law schools and medical schools, A&M institutions recruited the academically trained, rather than practitioners, for their faculty. In the early days the influence of classical scholars in the land-grant universities was so powerful that agriculture was frequently treated as an appendage of their primary responsibilities. At the Florida State College of Agriculture, one professor held a chair with combined responsibility for teaching agriculture, horticulture, and Greek; at Texas A&M, a doctor of divinity taught chemistry, natural science, and agriculture. The traditional academics often represented a major stumbling block to the expansion of practical agricultural education.[23]

In an effort to boost their standing, the A&Ms brought in basic scientists who set about building majors in their fields, attracting interested students, and hiring additional staff. Basic science lured students who frequently shifted their plans away from farming. The curriculum of the land-grant schools itself became more diversified and less geared to functional training, in response to both the changing interests of students and to the horizons of a more varied faculty. The transformation of many of these schools into state universities completed their turnaround from being single-purpose institutions.[24]

For all the limitations of narrow academic training as preparation for labor studies teaching, the alternative does not lie in glib proposals for giving "union experience" the major weight in the hiring process. The United Auto Workers, for example, has pushed to have its own union activists or retirees teach the courses they are promoting in community colleges. The UAW assumed, I think incorrectly, that knowledge of one industry could automatically be translated into knowledge of another unionized occupation or even into an understanding of labor relations in the national economy. Almost reflexively, university labor program directors insist on the importance of trade union background for successful teaching. The recently revised draft of the Rutgers statement on union-university cooperation urges that "instructional faculty, either for ad hoc or permanent positions, have significant labor organization experience to complement their academic training."[25]

Yet, an instructor in a new academic program with rich labor experience but limited credentials may find himself uncomfortable, if not intimidated, in a university setting. A faculty member who is a spokesman for a fragile degree often under attack by other departments should not be overawed by his opponents. One labor leader we spoke with about a possible academic appointment expressed reservations because he did not have a doctorate. Without this badge, he said, he would be an "apprentice" among a body of experienced journeymen. Ideally, labor centers should seek out candidates who combine union or social action experience with the necessary credentials. Unfortunately, there are fewer and fewer such individuals.

There are already indications that the backgrounds of labor faculty are changing. A recent survey conducted by the UCLEA of labor instructors at member institutions during the 1976–77 academic year uncovered the startling figure that 47.8 percent of the staff had no union experience.[26] Many veteran labor educators and trade unionists are muttering about "antilabor" attitudes and inexperience among the new recruits. If they are sour now, at a time when extension still dominates most labor institutes, they will become more so as degree programs take stronger hold.

As many of the old-time directors of university programs and staff step down, the style of the labor centers will surely change. The new leadership may be better credentialed, but it will lack many of the talents the old guard acquired from their union experience. Talents for bargaining, administration, and political infighting nurtured on union battlefields are gifts that veteran labor educators applied on the campus.

I have an image of MacKenzie, director of our center, plotting strategy for our degree as though he were in a union campaign. Like a bargainer, he guided us in making demands for our center while recognizing the need to make trade-offs if circumstances dictated. His careful attention to the small details—contracts, salary, promotion, working conditions— that make an employee's life easier stood out in my mind when I compared it to the cavalier attitude of my academic employers at State University of New York-College at Old Westbury. In their preoccupation with the abstract cause of workers, the supporters of labor studies on that Long Island campus rarely let themselves be distracted by the more modest concerns of the people who worked for them. The chairman of the American studies department once responded to my complaints about working conditions by saying that there always had been a little "exploitation" in the "movement."

The same tone carried over in the American studies department's approach to workers. When I proposed that we offer a certificate in our program, which is standard practice in university noncredit short courses, the chairman scoffed at the idea, as though it would be an artificial reward.

Labor Studies and Upward Mobility

Labor studies credit programs are certain to intensify the mobility tensions already latent in labor education. Unions will have much less control over the composition of classes and the aspirations of students than they do in extension arrangements. University policies forbid restricting admission to union members, which is the custom in short courses, conferences, and institutes. Courses are likely to mix trade union officials, government managers and labor relations staff, personnel from labor regulatory agencies, and younger, less experienced students seeking a path to labor jobs.

The heterogeneity of the degree courses bothers some university directors who have come out of the labor movement. Herbert Levine at Rutgers is trying to put a greater premium on "trade union experience" in admissions decisions in the master's program in labor studies. He is reacting to the large influx of management people to his program and to the small proportion of trade unionists—less than 45 percent in the first two years—in its early period of growth.[27]

The aspirations of the labor contingent are likely to change during their studies, just as prospective farmers altered their ambitions in the land-grant universities. Some union officials may decide to use their degree as a route to a management position, while others may change their minds and pursue a career in teaching or research. University programs would be strengthening a pattern that already exists, a process that takes skilled union staff from jobs at labor headquarters to new roles as Labor Department experts, arbitrators, consultants, and management negotiators. Public employees, prime beneficiaries of the degree programs, will, no doubt, maximize the opportunities for advancement that credit provides. A degree may make the difference between staying in a job under union jurisdiction and getting a position just a few steps up at the management level. The younger recruits to labor studies may see their preparation as equally valuable for a union job or for one on the management side. Some graduates of the oldest degree program, the one at the University of Massachusetts, have landed jobs as management representatives in government agencies.[28]

Even before the arrival of degree credit, labor educators faced the dilemma that successful training would tempt trade union leaders to leave the labor movement. Some of William Abbott's students in the programs he conducted for the Rubber Workers became so exhilarated about education that they left the rubber plants. A few became public school teachers. The more skilled a union member is in the tools of labor relations, the more valuable he is to management. One postal union official told me that he was frustrated that management would often tap the most competent stewards, the "grievance technicians," as another member of his union called them. The bestowal of degree credit creates additional incentives for leaving the organization.

Some veteran university labor educators bemoan the individualistic ethic they believe degree programs will instill. Mil Lieberthal, who is on the faculty of the Wisconsin School for Workers, critiqued the "academization" of the field in the *Labor Studies Journal*, the journal of the University and College Labor Education Association:

> where students earn an academic degree, and finding job opportunities limited, obtain work in organizations other than unions, they are then made middle class in occupation and outlook.

Academized labor education consequently will serve the middle-class, upwardly mobile, personal objectives of some members.[29]

The Parallel with Business

The history of the business schools offers a graphic illustration of the perils inherent in the drive for academic status. The rise of business training in colleges and universities was accompanied by the sloughing off of the vocational and trade school features that made it unacceptable as an academic discipline. The style adopted by business departments is one that labor programs will feel similar pressures to embrace.[30]

Before its transformation, business instruction was a response to the practical requirements of the marketplace. Teachers, who doubled as business practitioners, ran classes in commercial skills, such as accounting, bookkeeping, and office procedures. In his study of university business programs, Frank Pierson notes how tightly the academic and business worlds were linked:

> It was carried to its furthest extreme in the relationship between certain schools and societies of professional accountants. Indeed, it later became difficult to tell whether the accounting instructors in these schools were primarily teachers who had an accounting practice on the side, or primarily practicing accountants who wanted to keep their hand in the teaching profession.[31]

Business departments instituted reforms after 1955 that gave them greater standing in the academy. In the late 1950s, studies commissioned by the Carnegie and Ford foundations added to the urgency these programs already felt for change. The reports inveighed against the functional emphasis of their curriculum and recommended that vocational courses be shifted from undergraduate schools to the community colleges. They also urged that faculty be upgraded. Full-time instructors, one report argued, should replace ad hoc teachers, who "did not regard academic work as a full-time or major interest."[32]

The fruits of these recommendations were the vigorous efforts of business programs to tighten admissions requirements, to add graduate faculty, and to appoint faculty with better credentials. Following the lead of other departments, they made research a more important criteria in determining faculty promotions. The reformers added more general education courses and electives to the curriculum and generally weakened its vocational orientation.[33]

Business professors saw that the key to academic recognition was the formulation of a core of knowledge that would make their discipline unique. Weary of business's image as ancillary to economics or accounting, they made the analysis of decision making and administration central to "management science."[34]

Notes

1. Quoted in Margaret T. Hodgen, *Workers Education in England and the United States* (London: Kegan, Paul, French, Trubner, and Co., 1925), pp. 251–52.

2. Herbert Levine, "Union-University Cooperation in Labour Education," *Labour Education*, no. 30 (April 1976): 29; Herbert Levine, "Union-University and Inter-University Cooperation in Workers' Education in the United States," in International Labor Office, *The Role of Universities in Workers Education* (Geneva: 1974), p. 176.

3. Caroline F. Ware, *Labor Education in Universities* (New York: American Labor Education Service, 1946), p. 74.

4. Robert H. Wiebe, *The Search for Order* (New York: Hill and Wang, 1967), p. 127; see also Grant McConnell, *The Decline of Agrarian Democracy* (New York: Atheneum 1969), pp. 47, 176–77; Grant McConnell, *Private Power and American Democracy* (New York: Vintage, 1966), pp. 232–33.

5. "Effective Cooperation Between Universities and Unions in Labor Education," April 30, 1962, reprinted in Lawrence Rogin and Marjorie Rachlin, *Labor Education in the United States* (Washington, D.C.: National Institute of Labor Education, 1968), p. 273.

6. Ibid., pp. 274–75.

7. "University Labor Education Advisory Committees," AFL-CIO Education Department survey, February 1976, p. 2.

8. Interview with Dr. Herbert Levine, Washington, D.C., July 28, 1977.

9. "Summary of Proceedings 1976 Annual AFL-CIO Education Conference on Labor Education, Economics Education, and Women in the Labor Movement," Shoreham Americana Hotel, Washington, D.C., March 1–3, 1976.

10. Ibid., p. 9.

11. Ibid., p. 5.

12. Ibid., p. 17.

13. Ibid., p. 2.

14. In John R. MacKenzie, draft chap., "Labor Education in the United States," 1977, p. 3, the author contends that universities do 70 percent of the union training. This figure makes sense only if it includes the contributions made by colleges—in particular, community colleges.

15. Rogin and Rachlin, *Labor Education in the United States*, p. 3.

16. Richard Hofstadter, *Anti-Intellectualism in American Life* (New York: Vintage, 1963), p. 280; Richard Hofstadter and C. DeWitt Hardy, *The Development and Scope of Higher Education in the United States* (New York: Columbia University Press, 1952), p. 39.

17. Hilda Smith, "The Student and Teacher in Workers' Education," in Theodore Brameld (ed.), *Workers' Education in the United States* (New York: Harper Brothers, 1941), pp. 199–200.

18. Al Nash, "The University Labor Educator: A Marginal Occupation," *Industrial and Labor Relations Review* 32, no. 1 (October 1978): 49.

19. Interview with Dr. Herbert Levine, Bangor, Maine, April 7, 1977.

20. My understanding of the impulse of new vocations to raise their status in the academy has been shaped by my reading of Nathan Glazer, "The Schools of the Minor Professions," *Minerva* 12, no. 3 (July 1974): 346–64.

21. Ware, *Labor Education in Universities*, p. 8.

22. Glazer, "The Schools of the Minor Professions," p. 350.

23. Christopher Jencks and David Riesman, *The Academic Revolution* (Garden City, N.Y.: Anchor Books, 1969), p. 225; Hofstadter and Hardy, *Development and Scope of Higher Education*, pp. 40–41; Hofstadter, *Anti-Intellectualism in American Life*, p. 280.

24. Jencks and Riesman, *The Academic Revolution*, pp. 225–30.

25. "Joint Statement on Effective Cooperation Between Organized Labor and Higher Education," reprinted in *Labor Studies Journal* 1, no. 3 (Winter 1977): 293.

26. "Summary Report, Committee on Salary and Benefits, University and College Labor Education Association, 1976–1977 Academic Year," p. 3.

27. Interview with Dr. Herbert Levine, Washington.

28. See "Labor Relations and Research Center Roster of Graduates," University of Massachusetts at Amherst. This roster, one of the few bits of hard evidence on the career paths of labor studies graduates, covers the graduates of the program through June 1974.

29. Mil Lieberthal, "On the Academization of Labor Education," *Labor Studies Journal* 1, no. 3 (Winter 1977): 244.

30. For my discussion of business, I am indebted to Frank C. Pierson and others, *The Education of American Businessmen* (New York: McGraw-Hill, 1959), pp. 34–54, and to Earl F. Cheit, *The Useful Arts and the Liberal Tradition* (New York: McGraw-Hill, Carnegie Commission on Higher Education, 1975), pp. 83–107.

31. Pierson, *The Education of American Businessmen*, p. 41.

32. Quoted in Cheit, *The Useful Arts*, p. 100. On pp. 96–104, there is a useful discussion of the foundation-sponsored reports.

33. Ibid., pp. 104–5.

34. Ibid., pp. 105–6. See Robert L. Church, "Economists as Experts: The Rise of an Academic Profession in the United States 1870–1920," in Lawrence Stone (ed.), *The University in Society, Vol. 2: Europe, Scotland, and the United States from the 16th to the 20th Century* (Princeton: Princeton University Press, 1974), pp. 571–609, for an illuminating account of the transformation of economics into an academic discipline.

5

Union Staff and
Demand for Degrees

The increasing reliance on trained staff, a trend that cuts across all types of unions, has heightened the pressure for degrees. This development has tempered the trade union faith that the only qualified leadership comes up through the ranks. The number of operatives, organizers, business agents, joint board managers (union officials in the garment industry), and technical personnel from research, community services, legislative, and other union departments is spiraling. New interests have led unions to hire specialists in health and safety, polling, and the "quality of work life," efforts that provide greater self-determination for workers.

In his incisive study *Intellectuals in Labor Unions*, sociologist Harold Wilensky spotlighted, as early as 1959, the rising influence of the "professional service expert." The growing strength of these officials, Wilensky argues, reflected the premium placed by unions on technical proficiency rather than on organizing zeal. The professional service expert, the staffer most frequently to be found among the "facts and figures men" in research departments, was becoming the model toward whom other union officials were gravitating. While other personnel, such as the "party missionaries" and "legislative liberal missionaries," were altering their identities in the course of union service, Wilensky's investigation of career patterns showed that the professional service experts demonstrated remarkable stability.[1] These officials, who set their standards by the norms of their colleagues outside the union, were propelled by the "overall movement away from ideas and towards jobs, from a goal-centered outlook to a means-centered outlook."[2]

The most comprehensive survey of union hiring, conducted by Lois Gray, revealed that the majority of organizations recruit technicians who are not members. However, most tend to hire from their own leadership officials for the politically sensitive front-line positions in bargaining, organizing, and administration. The most surprising trend uncovered was that certain types of unions reached outside even to fill these posts. Unions with high-paid professional or technical membership with ample opportunities for advancement and those with poorly paid semiskilled or unskilled ranks were unique in their hiring practices.[3] Both AFTRA (American Federation of Television and Radio Artists) and SEIU (Service Employees International Union), which has a large membership of office-building workers and other low-paid employees, have sought such staff from outside their unions.

Another group of unions that breaks with the normal hiring patterns are those that are growing rapidly. Public-employee unions, like AFSCME, AFT, and NEA that are carrying on large-scale organizing, have an increasing need for talent that their own affiliates cannot supply. Within this growth sector of the labor movement labor studies programs will be able to find jobs for some of their graduates. The oldest program, the one at the University of Massachusetts–Amherst, has placed people in public employee organizations like the AFT, NEA, and NTEU, the fastest-growing federal government union. It has also found graduates jobs in the health care field, such as in state nurses associations, an area that has been ripe for labor organizing.[4]

Staff Training

The sharp changes in labor education—the growth of long-term and credit programs, the use of insights drawn from the social sciences, the functional style of the courses—in large degree mirror the priorities of the growing corps of union staff. One of the earliest university ventures in staff training, the nine-month residence program for officers and staff started at Harvard in 1942, was based on the assumption that union administration demanded management skills. Sumner Slichter, Harvard economist and the program's guiding spirit, contended that

> good administration is as desirable in labor unions as in business or government, and that it is altogether appropriate for Harvard to make available to trade union leaders the same type of training in administration that is offered to other groups, adapted of course to their needs.[5]

In 1955 Joseph Mire noted in *Labor Education* that universities were paying increasing attention to staff training:

> The more experienced institutions with full-time programs appear to have shifted the direction of their training from an almost exclusive emphasis on local union officers and rank and file members to substantial training programs for line and staff representatives.[6]

The largest staff training program today, the George Meany Center for Labor Studies in Silver Spring, Maryland, was conceived in 1969 "to develop trade union leadership through education programs in the social sciences and humanities in order that technical skills be buttressed by a firm grounding in theory and philosophy."[7] The center runs a year-round program of institutes for officials from AFL-CIO affiliates. Interunion courses have been offered in such areas as arbitration, health and safety, labor law, psychology for union leaders, and critical issues in state government.

More and more, however, the Meany Center has been asked to open its facilities to classes run by individual unions. Twenty-two unions carried on 28 institutes between April 1, 1976, and March 30, 1977. Even a building trades stalwart like the United Brotherhood of Carpenters requires all new business agents to attend a week-long program at the center. Close to 10 percent of that union's 2,000 business agents turn over every year.[8]

Staff training will also leave its imprint on degree programs in labor studies. While experienced people in union posts look to labor courses for upgrading, younger students will be eyeing credentials as an entree as staff jobs. After two labor studies courses and an internship at the city's labor relations department, one of my students leaped to a research job at AFSCME.

There are some indications that unions are starting to tap the university market in a systematic way. Unions will be sending representatives to Cornell to interview candidates for jobs. To enhance their appeal to union employers, who might otherwise turn to economics departments, journalism schools, and public health departments for staff, labor studies programs will undoubtedly face growing pressure to develop a more specialized curriculum.

THE ORIGINS OF THE FULLTIME UNION OFFICIAL

The great reliance on full-time staff rather than on unpaid leadership, which distinguishes American from European unions,[9] developed with the emergence of business unionism between 1890 and 1920 as the cornerstone of the labor movement. The definition of labor leadership as a salaried career reflected the ethos of a society that expected jobs to be based not on philanthropic incentives but on monetary rewards. The craft unions and early industrial unions of this period created positions that promised mobility for the ambitious wage earner. For the worker, the union post stood out as one of the few jobs of status that his social class allowed him.[10]

The role of the union office that the supporters of "pure and simple" trade unionism were shaping departed from the one embodied in the movements of labor reform, such as the Knights of Labor. The union was not all-consuming for the reformers. Terence Powderly, grand master workman for the Knights in 1882–83, also was simultaneously mayor of Scranton, Pennsylvania, county health officer, and operator of a coffee and tea business.[11]

The elevation of job control as the overriding mission of the union, which the reform labor movement had challenged, required business agents and other union officials to perform its central tasks. The crafts feared that social legislation in such areas as minimum wage and unemployment insurance would undermine their unions' appeal and make the leadership seem less indispensable. Consequently, they tried to preempt the state's role by a single-minded attention to collective bargaining. In addition to their bargaining responsibilities, the new officials, who were first employed in unions in local labor markets, policed agreements, organized new members, and supplied workers to a dispersed industry. The latter function, one of their most crucial tasks, made the business agent a middleman, a "small labor contractor," to use Robert Christie's description of the Carpenter's union official.[12]

By 1920, as unions made their first strides toward centralizing power at the national level, a better paid, more stable headquarters staff took office. This coincided with the capture of local power, with the growing control over strikes and bargaining by the national organizations. Unions began to hire organizers who were directly accountable to the national officers. The number of employees at some national unions was ballooning. In 1920 the United Mine Workers had 202 people on its payroll. Four years earlier it had such a large staff of traveling auditors that these officials could hold annual conventions.[13]

The arrival of "pure and simple" trade unionism was accompanied by a change in the flavor of leadership. Where labor reformers had stressed the assets of public speaking and journalistic skills, the talents of an educator, the new leaders accented technical knowledge and administrative abilities.[14] An article in the *United Mine Workers Journal* in 1910 describing an officer underlined the attributes of union leadership. It pictured the officer as a "walking budget of matters pertaining to the coal industry" and emphasized his "very good technical knowledge of coal mining."[15]

The major growth in union bureaucracy was dependent on the New Deal and, in particular, on the legal security and stability fostered by the National Labor Relations Act. The law, once a barrier to labor's advance, became a decisive instrument for union's gains during the Depression. The Wagner Act, passed in 1935, provided for elections sponsored by the National Labor Relations Board, the agency administering the law, to determine whether or not a union would represent the employees. A majority vote in its favor brought the union certification by the board. As a result, artful use of the legal machinery became more important than tests of force. This and other provisions of the act buttressed the union's power by investing the labor organization with legal rights. These reforms would make the trade union the axis of the labor movement, a movement once based on a diversity of organizations—labor parties, cooperatives, fraternal and reform groups.[16]

The industrial unions capitalized on the NLRB's machinery in their organizing campaigns in the mass-production plants. A favorable law coupled with the breakthroughs in bargaining opened up by World War II caused them to follow the example of the crafts. They, too, came to use full-time staff, such as organizers, economists, and representatives, to bring cases before the Board, the National War Labor Board, and other agencies.[17]

THE LABOR TECHNICIANS

The struggling unions of the 1930s have become powerful institutions. The former bands of organizers now operate from modern headquarters (the majority in Washington) with large staffs. Their treasuries are ample, their officers well paid. Unions administer large funds they have negotiated, such as pension, health and welfare, and training. Success has brought security and respectability. Recalled George Hardy, former president of the Service Employees International Union, one of the fastest growing unions in the AFL-CIO: "We don't have to meet in parking lots. We don't have to stand in the rain. We have offices, we have typewriters."[18]

Administration rather than organizing preoccupies many union leaders. Long-term contracts with a single company or a group of companies, particularly in the mass-production industries, have often created a three-year strike-free period. Time can now be spent consolidating gains, strengthening the contract through arbitration hearings, and administering the benefits. Legal recognition of the union shop, the requirement to join the union after a specified grace period as a condition of holding a job, and the deduction of dues by the employer have also produced stability. These devices freed labor from the chores of recruiting new members and generated the predictable cash flow on which union power rests.

Two former Steelworkers' staff members, Clinton Golden and Harold Ruttenberg, have written in telling terms of the effects of newly won prosperity and acceptability on the adversary role of union leaders.

John Witherspoon and Bud Barton, unlike many other belligerent union leaders, have become able contract administrators. Bud is more comfortable now in a suit coat and vest. John still likes his chew of tobacco, but he now wears coats that fit him and his appearance inspires confidence. The union has made them substantial citizens in their community. . . . They found that acting for the hates and grievances of a group of workers is easy. All they had to do, then, was to give vocal expression to the popular attitudes of the group. The job of giving the same group constructive guidance, often entailing unpopular acts, they found to be much more trying.[19]

The breadth and intricacy of the union agreement have weakened the position of the union generalist, the all-purpose organizer. Contracts that ran to two or three pages during the Depression are now voluminous documents covering such areas as grievance and arbitration procedures, seniority policies, cost-of-living formulas, and production standards. The specialist—the economist, lawyer, actuary, industrial engineer—now plays a pivotal role in the negotiation and administration of contracts. A headline in the *Detroit Times*, which appeared after the UAW guaranteed annual wage negotiations in 1955, captured the changes that had occurred: "From Brickbats to Briefcases: Ph.D.'s Do Bargaining for UAW-CIO."[20]

Fringe-benefit bargaining, which originated under the World War II wage and price controls as an ingenious way of providing benefits at deferred cost, brought experts to the forefront. Technicians handle fringes, which have blossomed from pensions, sick leave, and vacation clauses to include medical and dental coverage, supplementary unemployment benefits, and tuition refund plans.[21]

The international representative, the field officer from headquarters who assists the locals, will have to sharpen his skills just to keep up with the fine details of bargaining. Contacts with management officials confident in the specialized art of labor relations have fueled the drive of union officials for training. One student of mine, a local union officer, confessed that labor studies programs were needed so that labor's skills would not lag behind management's.

The most prominent of the union technicians in recent

years has been Lane Kirkland, who succeeded George Meany in 1980 as president of the AFL-CIO on his retirement. Kirkland's training was not classical, since he never held elected union office. His power came from his mastery of the skills needed to run a large organization and from his absorption in the details of labor relations and social policy. His apprenticeship included stints as assistant director of the AFL-CIO Department of Social Security, as research director of the International Union of Operating Engineers, as executive assistant to Mr. Meany specializing in speech writing, and finally as secretary-treasurer of the AFL-CIO. A former chief labor reporter for the *New York Times*, A. H. Raskin, observed that Kirkland's career epitomized changes in the labor movement:

> Kirkland's ascent to the summit reflects the emergence of a new breed of union leaders, a post-Depression, post-New Deal generation, whose vision of unionism is shaped less by memories of the sit-down strikes and private armies of scabs than by the administrative, technical, and legal headaches that go with managing computerized membership records, billions of dollars in reserve funds and year-round political action and lobbying machines.[22]

Union Staff and Collective Bargaining

The large number of individual, detailed agreements has also spurred the growth of full-time staff. Since the characteristic mode of bargaining in the United States is on an individual company or plant basis, agreements define wages, hours, benefits, and working conditions with considerable precision and detail. Broader agreements of the kind that span an entire industry or group of employers, which is the pattern in Europe, do not require a multitude of officials to negotiate, interpret, and police them.[23]

Multiemployer agreements, under which only 40 percent of American workers are covered,[24] are more common in Europe because of the prevalence of employer associations and of the control that labor federations frequently exert over bargaining. In the United States the AFL-CIO, a more decentralized organization than comparable European structures, does not interfere with the bargaining carried on by its affiliated unions.[25]

The ascendancy of the lawyer, the indispensable specialist in labor-management relations, springs from an economy in which an unfavorable contract may give one company an edge over another. Most American companies lack the protective mantle of the employer's association, a luxury their European counterparts enjoy. Detailed legislation, regulations, and case law grew up to set ground rules for the combative bargaining between enterprises. Although the law in the United States has left bargainers considerable room in determining the content of agreements, it has been firm in insisting that negotiating be carried on in "good faith," prohibiting such strategems as "take it or leave it" bargaining.[26]

Lawyers now play wider roles in unions, and some organizations use them to negotiate contracts. The American Postal Workers Union hired Bernard Cushman, a well-known labor lawyer, on a five-year contract to coordinate its negotiations and to be its chief spokesman in bargaining with the Postal Service. Lawyers bring arbitration cases for unions and have even been hired as organizers. In the federal government the dominant role of statute and regulations spurred the National Treasury Employees Union to hire many lawyers as business agents. The union is convinced that having staffers prepared to bring a lawsuit in a member's behalf is a primary selling point in its recruitment efforts.

The more centralized bargaining becomes, the more decisive the national union staffer's overall grasp of the industry will be to the forging and implementation of agreements. In the steel industry, the concentration of bargaining authority at national union headquarters propelled staffers like lawyer

Arthur Goldberg to positions of considerable influence.[27] The perspectives of local union leadership are less decisive than the determination of headquarters staff when national unions bargain for standard wage and benefit agreements for all the plants of a company or for an entire industry. The local union leader, whose knowledge is rooted to a considerable degree in his experience in one work place, frequently needs the national office representative to match wits with the industrial relations director from company headquarters.

Although local unions in the industrial sector have clung tenaciously to their powers, they have had to yield some of their prerogatives to their parent internationals. Unions in national product markets—auto, steel, rubber, electrical—share a common interest with employers in stabilizing labor costs throughout the industry. (Local unions have power to bargain over working conditions, such as health and safety, seniority, and work rules that are unique to their job site.) Not only wages but also fringe benefits demand the uniformity and efficient administration that national bargaining can produce.[28]

The urge to concentrate power, an impulse already strong among national unions, grows stronger with management's drive to centralize its operations. Unions tend to follow the lead of their corporate counterparts. As more unions merge to keep pace with the integrated structure of their industries or adapt their bargaining to conglomerate organizations, locals are apt to get further lost in the shuffle.

Even in industries made up of a large number of enterprises—men's and women's clothing, trucking, hotels and restaurants—business and labor have agreed on a strategy of centralized bargaining in which trained staff are essential. Fears of the ravages of unrestricted competition have sparked negotiations in which employer associations bargain with the union organizations, such as joint boards and councils representing locals in the industry. Full-time officials carry on the bargaining and contract administration for the locals that both sides hope will produce common wage rates and production costs.

Public-employee unions require a unique set of specialists: Their staffs must have a detailed knowledge of the budget process and the operations of civil service. The American Federation of Teachers local in New York City, headed by Albert Shanker, lured two city budget experts to its staff, William Scott, former first deputy city controller, and Laura Page, a budget analyst. Scott, the local's economics director and a top assistant to Shanker, was influential in shaping the final 1980 settlement agreed to by the coalition of municipal employee unions. Program Planners, Inc., the chief consultant to the Municipal Labor Committee in New York, created a major storm when it hired Allen Brauer, staff assistant to the director of the Budget Bureau. Mayor Ed Koch charged that Brauer's employment gave the unions access to confidential information, which would give them an unfair advantage in negotiations. District Council 37, the New York City affiliate of AFSCME, improved its command of pension policy, one of the most contentious issues in government-labor relations, by hiring Arthur Van Houten, formerly executive director of the New York City Employees Retirement Department.[29]

FEDERAL REGULATION

The expansion of federal regulation over matters that directly affect unions and the growing amount of legislation for which labor is lobbying have accentuated the centralization of expertise. The movement to Washington of national union offices with their large staffs, or the establishment of Washington offices by those headquartered elsewhere, shows how tied the trade union has become to the center of policy making, and not to its economic base.

Federal intervention brought about some of the earliest use of union staff. Past regulation, such as the World War I wage stabilization policy and the 1920 reorganization of the rail-roads, led needle trades and railway unions to hire experts. The proliferation of government agencies during the New Deal—the NLRB and the Social Security Administration, for example—led unions to hire researchers to prepare their cases before them.

Many of the "professional service experts" Harold Wilensky studied brought to their union jobs skills acquired in government jobs either during World War I or the New Deal. Some national officers whose background he examined used positions in the NRA as a stepping-stone to union leadership. Wilensky quotes one official on the advantages his NRA experience gave him:

> I'd done research with the NRA code authority. I learned more about the industry that way than I could possibly learn outside. Putting that together with the field contact, I was in a good position to know the industry and the union. . . . I'd been up in (city) for the NRA. . . . Having been up there before, I was more familiar with the complex political problems, the personalities of the leaders, as well as the economics of the thing. So when we negotiated the contract, I worked with the top officer on it.[30]

Now specialists are needed in Washington to fathom the reams of regulations issued by agencies like EEOC (Equal Employment Opportunity Commission) and OSHA (Occupational Safety and Health Administration). Others must be on call to assist local unions in meeting the reporting requirements demanded by the Landrum-Griffin Act (Labor-Management Reporting and Disclosure Act). The role of unions as lobbyists means that legislative staff must have knowledge of a great variety of issues—national health insurance, energy, transportation, and taxation, to name just a few.

The content of legislation has become so technical that labor is hiring staff, whose work for Congress helped them acquire the necessary proficiency. Three of the new people hired by the Legislative Department of the AFL-CIO have had Capitol Hill experience. The background of Howard

Marlowe, the department's new associate director, is representative of the new legislative experts. Marlow specialized in energy and transportation matters for Ruttenberg and Associates, a consulting firm that has assisted unions. A former political science teacher, he worked as a legislative aide for former Senator Vance Hartke.[31]

New Roles for Unions

The functions unions have assumed in providing a greater array of services to their members or in playing a broader role in the community demand managerial skills and technical expertise. Commissions and boards, such as manpower agencies, housing authorities, community service agencies, boards of trustees—seeking wider representation from the different interest groups have sought union representation. Unions jointly administer apprenticeship, training, and pension funds with management. The Amalgamated Clothing Workers own a bank and a housing project in New York City; the Carpenters' Union has retirement homes; and the AFL-CIO administers community service programs to counsel union members on the benefits for which they are eligible[32] such as unemployment compensation, welfare, food stamps, and health services.

Drawing on a sizable dues base, some large locals, the "welfare state locals," to use a phrase of Derek Bok and John Dunlop, have provided a network of services to their members. Local 668 of the Teamsters in St. Louis built a resort. Local 770 of the Retail Clerks in Los Angeles, which negotiated a comprehensive health plan, runs a health center that offers dental care, child and adult therapy, eye examinations, and other services. Harry Van Arsdale, president of Local 3 of the IBEW in New York City, enlarged the local's activities to include classes in critical thinking, arts programs at the union's auditorium, and a credit union.[33]

THE GARMENT UNIONS: PIONEERS
IN THE USE OF EXPERTISE

The use of technical knowledge by unions does not represent as sharp a departure from the past as it might appear. The terms of the trend are evident in the practices of the Amalgamated Clothing Workers Union and the International Ladies Garment Workers Union, two unions that contributed decisively to the tenor of the early workers' education movement. Ironically, it was these unions, both of which did so much to promote the concept of general education for the membership, that set the pattern of relying on specialists. Both saw the expert as the key to rationalizing the industry. Confronted with markets where savage competition was the rule, the needle-trade unions harnessed technical knowledge in the task of stabilizing their industries and enhancing their productivity.[34] Economist Richard Lester observed that the ACWU frequently played the role of "an industrial relations department for the industry," by curbing wage cutting, stopping competitive bidding among contractors, and promoting employer associations.[35]

To further his plan for bringing order to the men's clothing industry, Sidney Hillman, whom his biographer Matthew Josephson dubbed an "American Fabian," created the labor movement's first research department. Hillman named Dr. Leo Wolman, an economist recommended by Felix Frankfurther, to direct it. Hillman wanted Wolman to have a firm command of the diverse conditions in the industry and to amass the economic data pertinent to it. The Amalgamated pioneered in the use of permanent arbitrators, experts acceptable to both union and management, who resolved conflicts over such issues as production schedules and piece rates.[36]

Both the ILGWU and the ACWU welcomed the industrial engineers, much feared when in management's employ, to their staff to organize job evaluation, time study, and wage incentives. (The ILGWU was the first union to establish a department of industrial engineering.) Such experts, Hillman felt, would foster the efficiency that would produce increased wages and benefits for the union's members:

> We propose to make industrial science possible. We too shall employ experts familiar with all the devices of the stopwatch, etc. who will make time studies. . . . We are not opposed to methods of efficiency but they must be humanized and made subject to democratic control.[37]

Experts were also vital for handling the detailed tasks entailed in Hillman's program for "social unionism." They developed and administered the Amalgamated's unemployment insurance, housing, and banking projects. Their heavy dependence on expertise led the garment unions gradually to turn away from the traditional sources of talent they had drawn on in the Socialist movement. Consequently, president of the ILGWU David Dubinsky, wanted his union to establish a more formal training program:

> It is characteristic, too, that the gradual drying up of the old-type sources of leadership has run parallel with the profound changes in the old production patterns in our industry, which are also rapidly disappearing. The fact is that our employers are realizing the necessity of devising new methods and developing new craftsmen. . . .
> It is my opinion that our union must devise new methods and employ new techniques in the development of its future leadership; that it must sponsor an educational project and attract to it other sections of the labor movement in a labor college or such project for the purpose of training leadership for our union and for the trade union movement in general.[38]

The ILGWU Officers Training Institute, the fruition of Dubinsky's dream, started its program on May 1, 1950. As one staff member remarked, it fundamentally changed previous patterns of advancement in the organization:

The old way was to chisel your way in and make yourself indispensable. With the new training program, it's put on a practical, efficient basis. . . . It takes the guesswork out of it. There's careful selection and a specific preparation. The Training School is the modern equivalent of the YPSL and of course more . . . orderly and fair.[39]

Labor and the Intellectuals

Invaluable as expertise has become, we should not overstate its influence in an organization where political acumen still counts more than technical skills or credentials. Suspicion of intellectuals and wariness of university training as the best preparation for union leadership remains strong. Sidney and Beatrice Webb's vision of unions molding their staff along the lines of an independent civil service is far from realization.[40] Just at the time that credentialing for union jobs is on the rise, we find many trade unionists ardently invoking the tradition of rising from the ranks. Even in unions where college-trained staff has been important, patronage considerations can prevail over meritocratic principles. Staff openings in the Service Employees International Union, which has often hired graduates of the University of Massachusetts labor program, are scarcer because of the union's need to find posts for its defeated officers.[41]

Few technicians can expect to parlay their expertise, as Kirkland did, into positions of political power. Elected office, not an appointed staff job, has traditionally been the base from which policy-making authority is achieved. Only rare individuals, whose technical skills are complimented by organizational talents like negotiating ability, are able to rise to the top union posts.

Some lawyers have made good candidates for union office. Ralph Helstein, who became general counsel of the Packinghouse Workers in 1942, won the presidency of the union in 1946.[42] Jay Foreman, who was an attorney for the Retail

Clerks, holds the position of international vice-president in the newly merged United Food and Commercial Workers International Union. In its 1977 election for officers, the ILGWU named four men with law degrees to four of its five top offices.[43]

The foothold of the man of knowledge in unions is a fragile one. The trade union, although in the throes of modernization, still has many of the features of a political machine and a military organization. Wilensky describes the flux of the union, an institution in which clashing organizational styles vie for control:

> The union is at once a bureaucratic hierarchy and a body of faithful followers sometimes tied to the leader by a belief in his extraordinary personality or his mission, or more often by material interests.
>
> Political criteria and nepotism in recruitment; the absence of regularized salary structure, tenure systems, and promotion procedures; the fact that the role orientations of most experts deviate significantly from the model of the bureaucratic professional; the unexpectedly high influence of the Missionaries; an all-pervasive anti-intellectualism; the personal loyalty and pro-Labor imperatives, the crisis atmosphere and the demand for flexibility—these appear side by side with practices and attitudes that point to increasing formalization and routinization.[44]

The position of the intellectual in the labor movement is a dependent one. The university-trained staff member is resented at the same time that his special skills are most coveted. The labor leader, who rose to power from the shop floor, may feel that the college graduate is using his credentials to shortcut the established path to influence in the union. An individual with a variety of career options represents a threat to an executive whose opportunities for advancement are more limited, more subject to the unpredictability of union politics. The leader whose ascent to the heights of union office from a blue-collar job was swift may fall just as rapidly if he is defeated in an election.

The anti-intellectual strain in trade unionism, the stress placed on practical experience rather than theoretical knowledge, arises from the dominant role that bargaining, strike leadership, election campaigning, and other action-oriented functions play in the life of the union. One staffer interviewed by Wilensky caught the fast-breaking pace, the crisis-charged atmosphere, of union headquarters: "It's like a combination city desk, fire station and library."[45] Robert Hoxie, an early comentator on the labor movement, summed up its outlook incisively:

Labor leaders have been prone to act first and to formulate theories afterward, and . . . have acted habitually to meet problems thrust upon them by immediate circumstances.[46]

The union specialist's very remoteness from the center of action contributes to his subordinate position. The union leader is likely to place more stock in the advice of men involved in survival tasks like bargaining than in proposals formulated at some distance from the fray. Staff with the outgoing temperament and persuasive skills of the elected officer—the "contact men," the political and legislative technicians of Wilensky's profile—will have more headway with their boss than those who lack these traits. A gregarious politician is apt to be uncomfortable with the introspective manner of the union intellectual.

Labor chiefs worry that unless they keep tight rein on them union intellectuals' penchant for ideology and abstraction will cause dissension. Allowed too much discretion, they fear, the university-trained expert will push his own nostrums to the detriment of the union's bread-and-butter responsibilities. The battle between Brookwood Labor College and the AFL involved just this suspicion by organized labor of untamed ideology.

The distrust of intellectuals runs deeper than the facile denunciations of the learned, attacks that go back as far as Samuel Gompers's assault on the "professoriate . . . faddists, theorists, and effeminate men."[47] It comes out of a functional definition of trade unionism, a view most systematically expressed by Selig Perlman in his *A Theory of the Labor Movement*. In his opinion, and it is one widely held among unions today, the labor union could best tap the knowledge of the intellectual when it was applied to immediate, technical tasks. Perlman, who preferred the "social efficiency" intellectual, worried about the consequence of untrammeled exploration by intellectuals:

> So long as the intellectual is investigating specific subjects, which have definite and calculable bearings upon the workers' welfare,—for instance, industrial accidents, unemployment, wage trends, and the like—his tendency to reduce labor in the concrete to an abstraction is restrained. But let the intellectual's thought turn from relatively prosaic matters like the above to the infinitely more soul stirring one of "labor and the social order," and it is the rare intellectual who is able to withstand an onrush of overpowering social mysticism.[48]

The same devotion to expertise married to institutional objectives comes through in Perlman's remarks on the proper course for labor education:

> in order to carry on intelligent and effective collective bargaining as well as to stay organized, a considerable number of wage earners must be trained to be spokesmen of the group and the group as a whole must be trained to express itself in a rational and orderly manner. This means in terms of a concrete workers' education program the giving of classroom instruction in parliamentary law and public speaking, in labor economics, in labor history, and in related subjects.[49]

The suspicion of intellectuals creates a climate that intensifies the union professionals' isolation in the organization. Wilensky points out the constraints under which the typical staff member works:

The Internal Communications Specialist who is tempted to oversell either his version of the broad view or his specialty as the answer to all the union's problems, like all the staff experts, soon learns his place. If he fails to quiet down, if his orientation remains too "impractical," he is relegated to a peripheral position and ignored.[50]

To protect themselves, many staffers take pains to carve out a narrow area in which to function. Rather than risk embarrassment or criticism, they all too often take a backseat away from the policy-making arena. Some even adopt the fashionable anti-intellectualism of their organizations.

Others, for whom the union once was a vehicle for a larger social vision, carefully moderate their expectations. Even the expert with a commitment to research grows cynical when his product is bent to political ends. Self-depreciation is such a strong impulse among union intellectuals, some observers feel, that visions and ideas that might serve the labor movement are buried.

Russell Allen, deputy director of the George Meany Labor Studies Center and formerly education director of the Industrial Union Department of the AFL-CIO, underscores these perils:

> The danger is that the professional-intellectual will take so limited a view of his function that he will be content to perform routine tasks and will have no energy or will left over to provide the forceful advocacy of ideas which the movement also needs—that he will not be constantly pushing at the frontiers of union policies and actions.[51]

Unions and the Left

The events of the 1960s precipitated a rift between unions and intellectuals, particularly those active in movements for social change. The Left, which had traditionally looked to the labor movement as the engine of reform, began to dismiss it as a bastion of conservatism. The widespread support for the Vietnam War among unions, the AFL-CIO's reluctance to endorse George McGovern for President in 1972, and the federation's general wariness of the New Left strengthened the radicals' suspicions. The Civil Rights and Antiwar movements concentrated on organizing students and the poor, rather than workers.

Labor's leadership, including many in its reform wing, soured on the New Left as it moved from attacks on unions' complacency to an apparent disdain for even their limited objectives. Bargaining for wages and conditions were too mundane to arouse radical fervor. Several faculty members of the American studies department at the State University of New York College at Old Westbury, all movement veterans, for whom I worked organizing a labor studies program, would not deign to offer practical training to unions. Nothing short of enlisting workers in their favored social movements seemed to please them.

The different climate of the 1970s helped to heal some of these wounds. Mutual self-interest helped to build tentative alliances between labor and social-change organizations. Labor needs broad support to turn back the corporate offensive for a "union-free environment" and to repair its weakened position—for example, the decline in the union share of the work force, legislative defeats like the bid to reform the labor law, and its increasing losses in NLRB elections. The Left's condescension to labor's concerns began to fade with the growing awareness that its goals depend on widening its support. The movement leaders of the 1960s have left the campuses, and some have discovered trade union work as an outlet for their continued activism.

Enough committed young people have gotten jobs with unions to constitute what one journalist calls an "activist underground."[52] Unions actively organizing are drawing on the skills of movement leaders of the 1960s. Richard Rothstein, an early SDS community organizer, now directs the J. P. Stevens campaign for the Amalgamated Clothing and Textile Workers Union. Several of my college friends who were active in Civil Rights work are now involved in the labor movement. One of them, John Wilhelm, who helped establish an early community organizing project in the black community of New Haven, Connecticut, is now a business agent for the large Hotel and Restaurant Workers local in that city. More women and blacks will be filling leadership roles as labor struggles to build ties to constituencies underrepresented in its halls.

Even the Socialists have been the recipients of labor's goodwill. The Democratic Socialist Organizing Committee, which has a number of labor leaders among its members, including Jerry Wurf, president of AFSCME, Douglas Fraser, president of the UAW, and William Winpisinger, president of the IAM (the Machinists), has frequently offered assistance to trade unions. Most uncharacteristically, the Building Trades Department of the AFL-CIO ran an ad in the September 1979 issue of the DSOC newsletter lauding the organization for "its firm and militant support of the American labor movement."[53] The head of that department, Robert Georgine, gave a major address at the 1979 conference of the Democratic Agenda, an umbrella for social-change organizations started by DSOC.

The bewildering economic conditions of recession, inflation, and mounting layoffs have made some unions receptive to educational programs offered by Marxist economists. The Institute for Labor Education and Research in New York City has run classes on such themes as "What's Wrong with the Economy" for locals of CWA (Communication Workers of America), OCAW (Oil, Chemical, and Atomic Workers), IUE (International Union of Electrical Workers), and the UAW. The Summer Institute in Popular Economics, developed by Professor Samuel Bowles, one of America's leading radical economists, drew unionists to the University of Massachusetts-Amherst in 1979.[54]

Despite outward friendliness, labor organizations will expect contemporary activists (just as they did the radicals of the 1930s) to subordinate their visions to the demands of practical trade unionism—to the everyday tasks of bargaining, organizing, and handling grievances. The career of Jack Bigel, an old-left organizer and now a union consultant, demonstrates the kind of accommodations that make for survival in the labor movement. Bigel, who developed an extensive knowledge of city finance and, in particular, of fringe benefits in New York City, built a very successful union consulting firm, Program Planners Inc. Founded in the late 1950s, the firm serves as the adviser to the Municipal Labor Committee, the organization of the major nonuniformed unions. It was Bigel who masterminded the strategy in which the public-employee union pension funds staved off New York's financial collapse by purchasing $3.758 billion in city bonds. Bigel exerts a major influence on the unions' behalf in city labor negotiations.[55]

Bigel has traveled a considerable distance from his days as organizer and then as New York district president of the United Public Workers, a Left-oriented civil-service organization. He had worked as an investigator for the Welfare Department and was the guiding force of the public-employee labor movement in New York City during the 1940s. Once describing himself as a "mere technician," he has left his ideological commitments behind:

> I am not an anti-Marxist. I am not a Marxist. If I am anything, I would say I'm a pragmatist—as long as I've got to be an "ist." I have to be concerned with what we can do today, tomorrow, next year. I don't have any view about where humanity should go.[56]

Unions and Corporations: Contrasting Views of Knowledge

The contrast between the attitudes of the large corporations and those of labor on the use of knowledge is striking.

Corporations have been quicker to exploit comprehensive academic training for their staff and to take advantage of the fruits of social-science research.

In one illuminating study of extension programs conducted for unions and management by Cornell University in the New York metropolitan area, Al and May Nash discovered marked differences in their preferences for training. Unions typically requested courses specially designed for the needs of one organization. Business more commonly participated in courses attended by representatives of different enterprises. Of the management programs examined between April 1, 1965, and December 31, 1966, 64 percent were attended by such a mix; during the same period individual union programs accounted for 80 percent of the labor courses.[57]

Management programs more frequently borrowed perspectives from the social sciences than did union classes, which more often had a historical base. Unions more often sought out courses taught by practitioners—arbitrators, mediators, labor lawyers—than did management, which preferred faculty connected with a university or research institute.[58]

Although unions are gradually changing their assumptions about knowledge, they lack the spur to innovate that, as Derek Bok and John Dunlop suggest, the market provides the corporation:

> Unlike the typical business executive, the union leader is not goaded by market pressure, nor need he fear that his administrative shortcomings will be exposed in any balance sheet or market figures. As a result, unions will be slower to develop better methods of administration and organization, and successful innovations will be transmitted less rapidly throughout the labor movement than in the world of large corporations.[59]

The union, which still has many of the characteristics of a social institution, tries to shield itself from the market pressures that account for corporate dynamism. In one of the boldest attempts to account for the hold the union has on the emotions of its members, Frank Tannenbaum portrays it as a "society" that re-creates the cohesiveness and security workers have lost because of the atomizing power of industrialization. A traditional society, knit together in a fabric of "loyalties, values, rights, duties, privileges, and immunities," the union overcomes the isolation of the individual member in the market place:[60]

> In terms of the individual, the union returns to a worker his society. It gives him a fellowship, a part in a drama that he can understand, and life takes on meaning once again because he shares a value system common to others.[61]

The union employs the bargaining agreement to institutionalize the collective protections—seniority, grievance procedures, wage schedules—that check the unhampered operation of the market. In the hands of the union, a conservative force distrusted by 19th-century liberals and Marxists alike, the agreement curbs relationships based on "contract"—individual negotiations between worker and employer—and replaces them with those based on "status." This document, which builds heavily on precedent, on what unions term "past practices," can slow down the pace of corporate innovation.[62]

Labor economist Michael Piore has shown how difficult it is for employers to alter established wage relationships either among workers in one job category or between workers in different jobs. Custom, Piore says, is embodied in the contract and is so formidable in its influence on the work group as to be a competing force in the economy:

> In the modern work place, there is a dual allegiance to the morality of custom on the one hand and the individualistic ethic of the market place which sanctions management's pursuit of economic efficiency and the individual's pursuit of his own welfare on the other hand.[63]

UNION POLITICS AND EDUCATION

Political imperatives mold the way unions approach innovation-education. In contrast to the corporation, the union is preeminently a political institution. Douglas Fraser, president of the UAW, who narrowly missed being elected to that post previously, pinpointed one of the fundamental differences between these two institutions:

> This isn't like a big corporation, where a guy can be tapped and brought along in an orderly transition. You get through the system by being elected, and sometimes you can get shut out.[64]

Corporate leaders, unlike union executives, do not have a political base that they must constantly tend to. This partly explains the greater ease with which corporations can send their staff away for university training. Union officials fear that an extended absence may isolate them from a constituency that often resents schools for staff as "vacations." The George Meany Center for Labor Studies, which has the most extensive staff-training program, often has difficulty convincing labor leaders to come to its one-week residential schools. In the fall of 1980 the Meany Center will experiment to see if it can attract officials for a three-week course on organizing.[65] The trend has been for both unions and universities to conduct shorter staff-training programs.

Hierarchical as unions are, the best proposals and policies from headquarters may wither if the locals or intermediate bodies such as councils or districts choose to ignore them. A local leader who has his own constituency has more room to maneuver than does the staff of a large business enterprise. Bok and Dunlop shed light on the kinds of pressure tactics locals have at their disposal:

> The leader of a strong local, moreover, can also exert various forms of leverage not readily available in a corporation or government department; for example, he may threaten to oppose the administration at the next convention or even to pull his local out of the union entirely. He may passively resist the advice, admonition, or general direction of the national office, recognizing that busy general officers are unlikely to have the time or inclination to devote extended time to the affairs of a particular local except under extreme provocation. The dragging of local

feet frustrates more National union policies than any formal opposition.[66]

One union official I know expressed frustration over how little control he had over local and state bodies in his organization. He could set up regional conferences, but he had no way of requiring anyone to attend.

Most union leaders have an easier time justifying educational programs when they promise to fulfill political objectives. A program whose dividends are likely to be stronger morale and greater enthusiasm for union policies has more appeal than one with less measurable goals. Astute officers have used summer schools and other educational institutes as a way of doling out patronage. Since unions typically finance attendance at longer-term programs, a trip to summer school is one way of rewarding loyalists.

Classes can also be used to spot rank and filers with leadership qualities. J. B. S. Hardman, the first education director of the Amalgamated Clothing Workers Union, argued that labor education appealed most to union leaders when it operated as just such a proving ground:

> the new education-entertainment approach proved more appealing to union administrators. It attracts, they have held, the young, the mobile, and the not too sophisticated; the good mixers and the manageable. Observation of people in these activities should easily enable local leaders to discover those with apparent—or perhaps latent—qualities of mass appeal, those capable of carrying conviction and commanding a following. Singled out and given the needed polish and briefing, these would be the men and women the union needs as organizers and builders on the local level, not grumblers, fault finders, and disturbers.[67]

The political instincts of trade union educators make it hard for them to distinguish their teaching from their leadership roles. I noticed the dilemma among a group of educational staff from the American Postal Workers Union who participated in a teacher-training institute our center conducted in cooperation with their organization. I tried to encourage the representatives to emphasize the ambiguity of contract language in their educational programs, rather than insisting on pat answers to grievances. The union leaders were torn between the fear of losing face for not having definite answers to their members' questions and their desire as teachers to get them to think for themselves.

They were troubled by a role-playing exercise in which I assigned members of the workshop union and management positions on the private express statutes to act out. (They were to limit the involvement of commercial enterprises in delivering mail.) Such an exercise, some felt, would kindle doubts in their members instead of conveying an unequivocal union position. If a management view was role-played in a union class, it was argued, some members might be converted. For similar reasons, union leaders attending institutes cosponsored with a university often mistake conference evaluation forms, intended as educational tools, as a device to register unqualified support for the university labor center.

The lurking fear for the labor politician is that educational programs, if improperly handled, risk producing unrest in the organization and opposition to the leadership. One former educational director of an industrial union told me of the criticism leveled at him when graduates from one of his summer schools used their skills in parliamentary procedure against their union officers.

Even among leaders who are themselves the beneficiaries of labor training, education strikes a chord of apprehension. A group of newly elected officers, graduates of a community-college labor studies program, wanted the school to cut back its courses for fear that their rivals would capitalize on them. With variations, the themes of these stories recur when educators discuss the anxieties their work arouses among union officers.

Because of the political tempo of union life, education occupies a very low position among the organization's priorities. Before 1935 only three unions, all in the needle trades, employed full-time educational staffs. Only a quarter of the national and international unions—between 45 and 50—have substantial education departments. Among this number are such unions as the United Steelworkers of America, the International Association of Machinists, and the American Federation of State, County, and Municipal Employees.[68]

Since education is frequently not accepted as valuable in its own right, the education director may be shunted off to perform more pressing functions. Mark Starr, who was director of education for the ILGWU, talked of the perils he saw when education was subordinated to political or other organizational goals:

> In some unions the educational directors and staff serve as ward heelers for the administration. Their job is to see that their boss is re-elected. This attitude, of course, makes the educational staff and the classes nothing more than a yes-man chorus for the administration, destroying independence of thought and scientific inquiry.[69]

If the education director strays from the middle course to pursue an unpopular or innovative direction, he may find that the leadership of the union will try to restrict his path. The image one union education director drew of himself, that of a "beekeeper" fending off executive board members nipping at his side, neatly conveys the besieged feeling of these officials. Most trying of all, the labor educator has to compete with more urgent demands for the attention of the union leader. Bok and Dunlop explain how the climate of the union makes education a marginal activity:

> As in most political organizations, immediate problems and crises are constantly arising to attract attention away from the programs of a more intangible, long range importance. The time and effort of top union leaders are inexorably drawn from education programs into such tasks as bargaining, coordinating strikes, settling

local disputes, persuading subordinates in the field to take this or that course of action and curbing incipient revolts among segments of the membership.[70]

Notes

1. Harold L. Wilensky, *Intellectuals in Labor Unions* (Glencoe, Ill.: Free Press, 1956), pp. 161–66. Wilensky's study of the role of experts in the trade union organization is a superb one. His work has deeply influenced my own understanding of unions and the position of intellectuals in them.

2. Ibid., p. 166.

3. Lois Gray, "Trends in Selection and Training of International Union Staff: Implications for University and College Labor Education," *Labor Studies Journal* 5, no. 1 (Spring 1980): 13–15.

4. *Labor Relations and Research Center Roster of Graduates*, University of Massachusetts at Amherst, n.d.; Letter from Professor Harvey Friedman, director of the University of Massachusetts Labor Relations and Research Center to Joel S. Denker, May 20, 1970.

5. Caroline Ware, *Labor Education in Universities* (New York: American Labor Education Service, 1946), p. 24.

6. Joseph Mire, *Labor Education* (Inter-University Labor Education Committee, 1956), p. 71.

7. "Proposal for a National Labor Studies Center," prepared by AFL-CIO Department of Education, February 1969, p. 9.

8. Report to the Board of Trustees, George Meany Center for Labor Studies, Silver Spring, Maryland, April 20, 1977, *Summary and Comment;* talk by Russell Allen, deputy director, George Meany Center, to my graduate class, "Labor Education and Administration in the United States, March 17, 1977.

9. The great reliance by American unions on full-time staff is pointed out in Seymour Lipset, *First New Nation* (New York: Basic Books, 1963), p. 191. This volume contains an illuminating study of unions and their roots in American culture and compares them perceptively to their European counterparts.

10. In particular, the following works have influenced my treatment of the union official: David Brody, "Career Leadership and American Industrialism," in Frederic C. Jaher (ed.), *Age of Industrialism in America* (New York: Free Press, 1968), pp. 288–307; Seymour Lipset, *Political Man* (New York: Anchor Books, 1960), pp. 338–436; and Warren R. Van Tine, *The Making of the Labor Bureaucrat* (Amherst: University of Massachusetts Press, 1973).

11. Brody, "Career Leadership," p. 290.

12. Ibid., pp. 292–93, 295; Robert Christie, "The Carpenters: A Case in Point," in David Brody (ed.), *The American Labor Movement* (New York: Harper and Row, 1971), p. 50.

13. Van Tine, *Labor Bureaucrat*, pp. 75, 138, 143–44, 152.

14. Ibid., pp. 40, 54.

15. Ibid., p. 54.

16. The shrewd observation about the institutionalization of a once varied labor movement is made in David Montgomery, *Workers' Control in America* (New York: Cambridge University Press, 1979), p. 171.

17. Brody, "Career Leadership," pp. 299–300.

18. Quoted in William Serrin, "Labor Facing Major Challenges as It Plans for Leadership Shift," *New York Times*, November 15, 1979, p. 18.

19. Clinton Golden and Harold J. Ruttenberg, *The Dynamics of Industrial Democracy* (New York: Harper Brothers, 1942), pp. 57–58.

20. Quoted in Wilensky, *Intellectuals in Labor Unions*, p. 30.

21. Robert Tilove, "Pensions, Health, and Welfare Plans," in Lloyd Ulman (ed.), *Challenges to Collective Bargaining* (Englewood Cliffs, N.J.: Prentice-Hall, 1967), pp. 41–42, describes the origins of fringe-benefit bargaining. His essay is an excellent introduction, in lucid language, to a technical subject.

22. A. H. Raskin, "Lane Kirkland: New Style for Labor," *New York Times Magazine*, October 28, 1979, p. 9. Raskin's piece should be read not only for its portrait of Kirkland but also for its incisive analysis of issues facing the labor movement.

23. Derek C. Bok and John T. Dunlop, *Labor and the American Community* (New York: Simon and Schuster, 1970), pp. 208–9. The analysis of collective bargaining on pp. 207–28 is the most illuminating I have read.

24. Ibid., p. 208.

25. Ibid., pp. 52–53, p. 209.

26. Ibid., pp. 213–14.

27. Lloyd Ulman, *The Government of the Steelworkers' Union* (New York: John Wiley & Sons, 1962), p. 73.

28. Arnold R. Weber, "Stability and Change in the Structure of Collective Bargaining," in Ulman, *Steelworkers' Union*, pp. 13–36, has as one of its major themes the centralization of collective bargaining in the United States.

29. William Serrin, "Shanker Juggles Politics and Contracts," *New York Times*, July 11, 1980, B–2; Ken Auletta, *The Streets Were Paved with Gold* (New York: Vintage, 1980), pp. 320–21.

30. Wilensky, *Intellectuals in Labor Unions*, p. 27, describes the impact of early federal regulation on the use of union staff. Wilensky quotes this official as part of his intriguing account of the backgrounds of union staff, p. 214.

31. James W. Singer, "Labor Lobbyists Go on the Defensive as Political Environment Turns Hostile," *National Journal* 12, no. 11 (March 15, 1980): 443.

32. See William Abbott, "Effective Union Administration," pamphlet, Industrial Relations Center, College of Business Administration, University of Hawaii, Honolulu, April 1967, especially pp. 33, 56, for insights into the broader role unions can play.

33. Bok and Dunlop, *Labor and the American Community*, pp. 375–77.

34. Richard A. Lester, *As Unions Mature* (Princeton: Princeton University Press, 1958), pp. 90–91. Daniel Bell, *The End of Ideology* (New York: Free Press, 1962), p. 213, discusses the stabilizing role of the garment unions in his analysis of "market unionism."

35. Lester, *As Unions Mature*, p. 91.

36. Matthew Josephson, *Sidney Hillman: Statesman of American Labor* (Garden City, N.Y.: Doubleday, 1952), an exciting biography, discusses Hillman's fascination with expertise.

37. Ibid., p. 197.

38. Quoted in Mark Starr, "Training for Union Service" in J. B. S. Hardman and Maurice F. Neufeld (eds.), *The House of Labor* (New York: Prentice-Hall, 1951), pp. 443–44.

39. Quoted in Wilensky, *Intellectuals in Labor Unions*, p. 254.

40. See ibid., p. 19, for reference to the Webb's vision of trade unions.

41. Letter from Professor Harvey Friedman to Joel S. Denker.

42. Wilensky, *Intellectuals in Labor Unions*, p. 216.

43. A. H. Raskin, "Unions Turning to the Law and College for Top Officials," *New York Times*, June 22, 1977, pp. 47, 53.

44. Ibid., p. 276.

45. Ibid., p. 276.

46. Quoted in J. David Greenstone, *Labor in American Politics* (New York: Vintage, 1969), p. 53.

47. Quoted in Richard Hofstadter, *Anti-Intellectualism in American Life* (New York: Vintage, 1963), p. 285.

48. Selig Perlman, *A Theory of the Labor Movement* (New York: Macmillan, 1928), pp. 280–81.

49. Quoted in Ernest E. Schwartztrauber, *Workers Education: A Wisconsin Experiment* (Madison, University of Wisconsin Press, 1942), p. 126.

Wilensky, *Intellectuals in Labor Unions*, p. 102.

51. Russell Allen, "The Professional in Unions and His Educational Preparation," *Industrial and Labor Relations Review*, October 1962, p. 24.

52. See "Young-Turk Network: New Force in Unions," *U.S. News and World Report*, March 19, 1979, pp. 79–80.

53. "Socialism is no longer a dirty word to labor," *Business Week*, September 24, 1979, p. 130.

54. See Robert Magnuson, "Lessons in Socialism at a School for Labor Leaders," *New York Times Magazine*, August 12, 1979, F–3.

55. For background on Bigel's career, see James Ring Adams and Daniel Hertzberg, "New York's Ranking Power Broker," *Wall Street Journal*, March 7, 1979, p. 20; Lee Dembart, "Jack Bigel Holds Many Keys to City's Mansions," *New York Times*, December 11, 1976, p. 25;

Vivian Gornick, "Jack Bigel: A Marxist Among the Millionares," *Village Voice*, November 8, 1976, pp. 26, 28, 31.

56. Gornick, "Jack Bigel," p. 26.

57. Al Nash and May Nash, *Labor Unions and Labor Education*, University Labor Education Association, Monograph Series, no. 1, June 1970, pp. 9, 13.

58. Ibid., pp. 11–12.

59. Bok and Dunlop, *Labor and the American Community*, pp. 187–88.

60. Frank Tannenbaum, *A Philosophy of Labor* (New York: Alfred A. Knopf, 1951), pp. 3–13, 59–78, 143.

61. Ibid., p. 10.

62. Ibid., pp. 49–57, 79–100, 138–54.

63. Michael J. Piore, "Fragments of a 'Sociological' Theory of Wages," *The American Economic Review* 63 no. 2, (May 1973): 378.

64. Charles B. Camp, "UAW's Doug Fraser is Due to Lead Union in an Era of Changes," *The Wall Street Journal*, January 26, 1977, p. 28.

65. Interview with Russell Allen, Silver Spring, Maryland, June 3, 1980.

66. Bok and Dunlop, *Labor and the American Community*, p. 152.

67. J. B. S. Hardman, "Labor Education a Complicated Thing," in J. B. S. Hardman and Maurice F. Neufeld (eds.), *The House of Labor* (New York: Prentice-Hall, 1951), p. 477.

68. John R. MacKenzie, draft chap., "Labor Education in the United States," 1977, pp. 2–3.

69. Mark Starr, "The Task and Problems of Workers Education," in Hardman and Neufeld, *The House of Labor*, p. 426.

70. Bok and Dunlop, *Labor and the American Community*, p. 185.

6

Union Outlooks on Labor Studies

On the surface, the growth of labor studies seems to be inexorable. On closer examination, however, its development appears to be filled with tensions, signifying the divided feelings among unions and their members about this phenomenon. Even the staunch supporters of labor studies among union leaders recognize that it is not uniformly popular among their rank and file. Officers and union activists will enter college because of the attraction of labor studies courses. But many members will seek further education for altogether different reasons. They may pursue a degree in order to achieve a dream of mobility, to satisfy a need for self-esteem, or to have a general education. The dilemma labor educators are experiencing is about how to respond to those impulses while maintaining the rank and filer's loyalty to the union.

The Building-Trade Unions

Despite all the indicators of enthusiasm, the growth of labor studies is following a more tentative course in several major sections of the union movement. Building-trade unions, the stereotyped foes of education, have been leaders in the drive to establish degree programs for their members. Their efforts, however, have not been focused on labor studies, but on raising the standing of apprenticeship and on providing an avenue for the craftsman's striving for upward mobility. Only recently have plans developed to introduce a labor studies core into the two-year degree programs that have been constructed on an apprenticeship base.

More unions are involved with apprenticeship programs than with any other activity on community college campuses. A recent survey indicates that the International Brotherhood of Electrical Workers (113 programs), the Plumbers (73), the Sheet Metal Workers (40), and Machinists (38) are the leading unions in relying on this, the most common form of labor–community college cooperation.[1]

Building on this relationship, some of the skilled trades have established "dual enrollment" programs that credential apprenticeship programs. They grant credit for the instruction conducted by the labor-management apprentice committees and add those courses, such as English and social studies, that are necessary for a two-year degree. The reward for the student is both an associate degree and a journeyman's card.[2]

The idea of using apprenticeship as a base on which to build a degree has taken hold in those crafts most attuned to the disorienting impact of technology on their occupations. An overwhelming number of first-, second-, and third-year apprentices polled by the IBEW said they wanted to get a degree. This union has members revising textbooks to keep up with changes in the electronics field and is using community colleges to retrain their journeymen.[3]

The Operating Engineers, a union whose current and former president had college degrees and whose membership has become increasingly better educated, were pioneers in dual enrollment. It viewed the experiment in part as a way to earn academic respect for its apprenticeship programs. The assistant director of its education department, A. Michael Collins, argued:

> The College personnel are encouraged to view the curriculum as a whole course of study in itself, not as bits and pieces that would be "equivalent to" particular existing courses, not as a "direction" in mechanical engineering or a "branch" of civil engineering but a career field in itself, with rich possibilities for further exploration.[4]

Dual enrollment, the Engineers believed, also offered an avenue of opportunity for the building tradesman who did not want to be locked into his job. A two-year degree might open a path to a management position in the construction industry or serve as a stepping-stone to a four-year diploma and a new career.[5] The contractors also supported the idea. Management could select the graduates of the programs as candidates for supervisory jobs.[6]

Apparently in an effort to counteract the technical focus of dual enrollment and its emphasis on individual advancement, Reese Hammond, education director of the Operating Engineers, proposed that the U.S. Department of Labor support the development of a labor studies curriculum for these degrees. The agency agreed to fund the George Meany Center for Labor Studies to develop pilot programs at four community colleges. These two-year A.A. degrees will offer a major in labor studies while continuing to provide credit for apprenticeship training. The grant also pays for the writing of labor studies texts and for training faculty to teach in the new programs.[7]

The Public-Employee Unions

The unionized group that can turn credit most effectively to its advantage are the public employees. If industrial unions were the cutting edge of labor education in the past, future programs are likely to bear the imprint of government workers. Yet civil-service unions, and the labor education programs eager to reach their membership, are pulled in seemingly contradictory directions: on the one hand, toward encouraging the rank and file's desire for job advancement and, on the other, toward building interest in their unions.

Just as the organizing drives in the mass-production industries—in auto, electrical, steel, and rubber during the 1930s and 1940s—were responsible for the momentum in the labor movement, so today the most rapid growth in union membership is taking place among public school teachers, college professors, city workers of all kinds, hospital employees, caseworkers, and other public employees. The areas of greatest union strength in the past, such as manufacturing and transportation, are either largely organized or are in stagnating, if not shrinking, sectors of the economy. The contraction in the economic base of the private-sector unions is reflected graphically in the declining proportion of the work force holding union cards. The proportion of nonagricultural workers organized today is lower than it was at the end of World War II.[8]

While the industrial unions are losing strength, public-employee unions are expanding their membership and increasing their share of the government work force. Between 1974 and 1976 membership in state and local government unions rose from 1.5 to 1.7 million. More than half of all such workers are on their rolls.[9] (Through exclusive bargaining agreements they represent far more.)

Two unions in particular are outstripping the organizations representing employees in the private sector. The American Federation of State, County, and Municipal Employees, which has been adding 5,000 members a month, has grown to more than 750,000 members. The National Education Association, the largest of the burgeoning civil-service organizations, recruited 200,000 new members between 1974 and 1976 and is now second only to the Teamsters in membership.[10]

The public-employee unions have made these gains against

heavy odds. Many of the legal protections, weak as they may be, that private-sector unions routinely expect are unavailable to government workers. Public employees are not covered by the National Labor Relations Act or by most major protective legislation—the minimum wage law, for example. The courts have erected barriers that block equal treatment for them, barriers whose harshness recalls the legal obstacles that unions in the private sector struggled to surmount. The major blow came in the 1976 Supreme Court decision *(National League of Cities et al. v. Usery, Secretary of Labor)* that struck down the extension of minimum wage and maximum hour protections to state and local government workers.[11] "State sovereignty," the Court said, forbade Congress from exercising this power under the commerce clause.

If the same assumptions prevail, the Court is certain to invalidate a federal collective-bargaining law for public employees. Without the security of a national law, government workers have had to fall back on city councils and state legislatures for protection. The reluctance of citizens to pay higher taxes for public-employee benefits, a backlash almost unknown in the buoyant economy of the 1960s, has put these unions even further on the defensive.[12]

Restrictions on their right to negotiate a union shop, to bargain for wages (in the federal government), and to strike hamper their ability to expand their membership and to exert maximum pressure on their employers. Even when negotiations are permitted, public management often succeeds in limiting the range of subjects on the bargaining table. Civil-service laws and agency regulations, some public managers have asserted, are inviolable, and collective bargaining agreements cannot modify them. Some states have spelled out in statute specific areas of management authority with which collective bargaining is forbidden to interfere, such as "mission of the agency" and "inherent managerial policy."[13]

Executive Order 11491, which established limited collective bargaining in the federal government in 1969, contained a "management rights" section that has influenced similar provisions in cities and states:

> management officials of the agency retain the right, in accordance with applicable laws and regulations: (1) to direct employees of the agency; (2) to hire, promote, transfer, assign, and retain employees within the agency, and to suspend, demote, discharge, or take other disciplinary action against employees; (3) to relieve employees from duties because of lack of work or for other legitimate reasons; (4) to maintain the efficiency of the Government operations entrusted to them; (5) to determine the methods, means, and personnel by which such operations are to be conducted.[14]

Even when constraints on public employees have been relaxed, the weight of past paternalism still influences workers and their union representatives. Throughout the short course I taught for Local 2095 AFSCME, the local at St. Elizabeth's Hospital, I had to reassure the union leadership of their right to "negotiate," rather than merely to "meet and confer," over a great variety of working conditions, such as scheduling, parking, and staff-patient ratio. I was trying to suggest that, even though the local could not negotiate personnel policies and other government regulations per se, they could bargain about the effect of these actions on the work force.

The officers felt instinctively that they could negotiate these matters, but they feared that the Federal Personnel Manual, civil-service rules, or agency regulations prohibited it. The union staff member assisting the local typically deferred to "higher" standards. When I suggested a new negotiating tack or contract proposal, he sometimes asked whether "civil service" would permit it. A union in the private sector, in contrast, would try to break as much new ground in negotiations as management would agree to. Only if a specific line of bargaining were explicitly forbidden would such a union withdraw a demand.

As new locals spring up as a result of successful organizing drives or as state laws grant new rights to government workers, public-employee unions frequently discover that they have an urgent need for training. Either through their own union or nearby state university, they take classes to learn how to cope better with the responsibilities that recognition or their new legal status have thrust upon them. Commonly, civil-service unions seek training in union administration, collective bargaining, and other organization-building skills. Skills in these areas are so scarce that these unions have asked for more classes than understaffed university labor centers can possibly supply.[15]

Faced with very similar demands, industrial unions developed leadership training programs. Using the machinery of the National Labor Relations Act and their own organizational talents, the mass production unions built up countless locals in large industrial plants. These locals needed trained stewards, committeemen, and union officers. The voluntary local leader on the shop floor, rather than the business agent the crafts depended on, played the key role in handling grievances and carrying on other representation functions.

As William Abbott, former education director of the United Rubber Workers, has argued incisively, local education in the industrial union was an attractive way of offering some autonomy to workers whose jobs held little such promise:

> How many auto workers could find self-fulfillment in the rasping whirr of an assembly line? But an unpaid shop steward helping one's fellow workers to right wrongs in the shop was self-actualizing. The human value craftsmen found in their work could be discovered through union activity in a steel mill or in a rubber plant. "Education" to many industrial unionists meant learning to be better grievance handlers, bargainers, or union administrators. This kind of training was called "labor education" and unions developed education programs of their own or went to colleges and universities for help.[16]

Labor education on the lines of the industrial union model is likely to be just one dimension of the training programs public-employee unions offer their members. The government worker has mobility routes open to him other than a union post. While an industrial worker might use an educational program to advance himself in his organization, the public employee can use training to attain a better job, a rise in step or grade in the civil service, or more pay. Management's willingness to pay for training and to offer workers time off for education provides another inducement.

A "supervisory" position, a classification with less authority (such as power to fire) in the public than in the private sector, looks far less remote to a lower-level government worker than to a factory worker. (Public-employee unions have frequently represented supervisors in the same bargaining unit with their subordinates or in a separate unit).[17]

The most ambitious response by a public-employee union to the membership's pursuit of credentials is the multifaceted educational program run by District Council 37, AFSCME, in New York City. The council, directed by Victor Gotbaum, has been aptly described as a "way of life union": Its range of services to members include a family activities program, a childrens' activity center, and a retirees' program.[18]

The union's initial venture in training was a program begun in 1967 to upgrade nurses aides to licensed practical nurses. One headline in the council's newspaper cheered the opportunities for advancement the classes offered: "Learn, Baby, learn—to earn, baby, earn . . . Learn to earn program for hospital aides brings cash and careers to thousands." In 1969 it negotiated an educational trust fund based on a fixed payment per member contributed by the city. The organization now has a $1.5 million annual education fund that it can tap to provide services to the 60,000 bargaining unit members.[19] Confronted with rigid administration of the fund, the council wrested control of it from the New York City Department of Personnel in 1970 negotiations. The adeptness the council showed in its struggles with the personnel department illustrates the cogent observation of Sterlin Spero and John Capozolla on training in the public sector:

> Personnel departments no longer possess the autonomy or discretion they once had in the area of training. Unions will tend to emerge as an equal partner if not a "major stockholder" in training, promotion, and career development programs.[20]

The union has devised a host of services to assist members in taking full advantage of the training fund. Counselors are available to help workers plot a career path, and there are classes to prime them in the reading, writing, and speaking skills they will need for college. Members can enroll in a high-school equivalency course or take classes on how to pass civil-service exams. These programs are especially attractive to members because they are run from the union's headquarters in lower Manhattan, where many members live.[21] The training fund provides $450 a year to each member for tuition expenses. Monies are available immediately rather than upon completion of the courses, as is the case in many tuition refund plans.[22] With these resources the union has worked out agreements with colleges to provide career-oriented courses. These courses must award credit so that members can use them to gain promotions.

Promoting upward mobility lies at the heart of the council's own college, an undergraduate division of New Rochelle College based at union headquarters. The "Downtown Campus of District 37," which runs an interdisciplinary program, developed in part from the demands of the graduates of the union's high-school equivalency program for additional educational opportunities.[23] Labor studies is a small part of the New Rochelle program. The majors in the social services and in management, for example, which offer workers a means of advancement in their agencies—from clerk to social worker or to supervisor—are considerably more popular.

Members are drawn to this undergraduate degree out of a drive to advance in their jobs, rather than to rise in their unions. A suggestive study of the New Rochelle program found that 75 percent of the students were women in their forties from minority backgrounds who worked as secretaries or in other clerical jobs. They saw the college degree as a vehicle for improving their employment. The members of the largely private-sector student body in Cornell's Labor–Liberal Arts Program, on the other hand, were more apt to see the program as a way to improve their position in the union. (The study, in fact, determined that a large proportion of the Labor–Liberal Arts graduates attained new positions in their organizations.)[24] Council 37's encouragement of its members' ambitions is so unstinting that it conflicts with its organizational interests. Educational success may propel members out of the bargaining unit. (This happened in the program that trained about 400 nurses aides to become licensed practical nurses.)[25]

A credential that promises pay increments or job advancement can be the sweetener that makes a labor-oriented curriculum attractive to government unionists. A stream of credit-conscious government workers is helping accelerate the growth of labor studies programs. The brisk unionization of teachers in New Jersey pushed the Rutgers labor program to start labor education majors in both the master's and doctorate curricula of the university's School of Education.[26]

If the experience of the Labor College in New York is an accurate barometer, similar programs can count on recruiting large numbers of civil-service workers. Between 1973 and 1976 the composition of the student body in that institution changed dramatically. During that period it attracted a greater percentage of students who were younger, rank and file, white-collar, and with some college education. In 1976 vocational teachers, school secretaries, and clerical workers comprised most of the white-collar contingent.[27] This represents a pronounced change in an institution that got its initial push from a building-trades union, Local 3 of the International Brotherhood of Electrical Workers. Two organizations of government workers, the United Federation of Teachers and the Civil Service Employees Association, accounted for 54 percent of the students who were union members that year— 29 percent and 25 percent, respectively.[28]

Larger numbers of public employees in labor studies classes will alter their curriculum. More courses with a "public administration" orientation will appear: for example, our proposed course entitled "State and Local Government Collective Bargaining: Its Relationship to Taxation and Finance." Classes dealing with the management and finance of government programs will spring up in response to the larger policy-making role of these unions.

Aggressive negotiations by unions and associations, in particular those representing service workers such as nurses, teachers, caseworkers, and firemen, have won them a share in powers that traditionally have been reserved for management. Teachers' unions have won contracts with clauses spelling out class size, the school calendar, and the right of faculty to participate in decisions on textbooks and curriculum. Caseworkers have negotiated agreements specifying maximum case loads.[29] The hospital workers I taught from St. Elizabeth wanted a clause in their contract on staff-patient ratios. If there were too few workers on a shift, any one of them could be in serious danger. My class remembered that a deranged patient had killed one of their coworkers.

The tradition of "meet and confer" in the civil service, of informal agreements and understandings, has frequently crumbled under the pressure of tough bargaining. Union negotiators often do not distinguish between "working conditions" and "management rights." Effective administration of services is often so dependent on the use of manpower that wrangling over "working conditions" quickly turns into bargaining about policy.

Public managers, who do not feel the intense market pressures of their counterparts in private industry, have often been willing to yield ground to the union. Sterling Spero and

John M. Capozzola, two students of state and local government, discern this trend toward "codetermination" and worry that the management function will weaken under its pressure:

> All employer-employee relationships are not rooted in collective bargaining. Consultation, accompanied by informal understandings, is a way in which to handle issues where responsibility for decision rests with legally designated public authorities.
>
> Consultative practices have proved to be mutually satisfactory and educative. If adopted by local governments, consultative machinery could enhance legitimate managerial authority and give employees a constructive role without interference with the function of management to establish and control policy.[30]

The fiscal crisis plaguing many cities gives the public-employee union an additional incentive to acquire knowledge of public administration. When a wage freeze was instituted in New York City that permitted only cost-of-living increases provided by greater productivity, the public-employee unions recognized that efficient management was in their self-interest. A city-wide labor-management committee was established to promote work-place efficiency, including changes in work rules and staffing patterns. Victor Gotbaum, the Council 37 leader who has been keenly interested in productivity decision making, instituted 40 labor-management committees in city agencies. Improvements in efficiency produced by this mechanism, the council contended, saved the city nearly $8 million.[31]

New York's reliance on public-employee pension funds to purchase bonds to forestall default (more than one-third of their investments are in municipal securities) has given the organizations additional leverage over policy making.[32] The more widespread labor-management committees and other forms of joint decision making become in the public sector, the more likely it is that courses in managerial skills, budget analysis, and policy making will be added to the labor studies curriculum. If their participation in management is to be more than a nominal one, union staff will need to have a firm grasp of these areas.

Public-employee leaders are bound to insist that labor studies courses address legislative issues that are important to their organizations. The recognition that the problems of their members in the cities and states were intertwined with national social policy has spurred the interest of the civil-service unions in new legislation. The reforms unions like AFSCME have been pushing—tax reform, revenue sharing, welfare reform, countercyclical spending—would bring an infusion of funds for programs, facilities, wages, and staff.

Industrial unions, the bulwark of past labor education programs, won protections from Congress, such as wage and hour legislation and social security and unemployment regulations, that could not be achieved through collective bargaining. The classes these organizations sponsored for their members highlighted their legislative priorities.

The Industrial Unions

The demand for credit among industrial union members is also made up of conflicting elements. Promoters of labor studies in these unions will have to compete with the other interests and aspirations of their members.

The tuition-refund plans these unions have negotiated have forced them to make decisions on what should qualify as reimbursable training. In the forefront of this innovation is the United Auto Workers, which commits more of its resources (between 6 and 7 percent of total income) to education than any other American union.[33] The union, whose constitution requires that locals set up education committees and earmark dues money for educational programs, employs 18 educational representatives to service its members (one for each region). It runs a wide range of classes for its rank and file, officers, and staff, including short courses, regional conferences, and summer schools. Three family education centers, the most spacious and equipped of which is at Black Lake, Michigan, provide both instruction and recreation to husbands, wives, and children during the summer.

Eighty-five percent of the UAW's members (they must be seniority employees) are covered by agreements, which will reimburse them up to a maximum of $900 annually.[34] The UAW, which first negotiated tuition refunds in 1964, agreed with the company on the priority of "job-related" training.[35] These benefits, whether employer-initiated or authorized through union contract, have largely developed in high-technology enterprises like the auto companies.[36] The interests of industrial unions in developing new skill levels among their members through upgrading and retraining coincide with management goals. The tuition-refund programs in the auto industry limited eligible courses to those that were "job related"—to "courses which improve your present job skills . . . that relate to the 'next' job in the logical development of your career as an employee with your company . . . that can prepare you for 'job openings' that are expected to occur in the future."[37]

Both craft and industrial unions, many of which have sizable skilled-trades departments, spend heavily on technical training. These unions and their supporting organizations received more than $185 million from the Department of Labor between 1963 and 1976 for manpower programs, such as Job Corps, Apprenticeship Outreach Program, and National On-the-Job Training Programs.[38]

The Education Department of the UAW recently seized on the tuition-refund provision as a vehicle to enlist more members in the community-college labor studies programs that it was developing. Noncredit labor education programs, former UAW Education Director Carroll Hutton stated at a conference of the University and College Education Association, were reaching a saturation point: "They're [the union members] drowning in non-credit programs."[39]

Union students in certificate programs were looking for an avenue to continue their studies. In 1966 the union took a survey of 110 students, almost all members of the UAW, in the third and fourth semesters of Wayne State University's noncredit labor program and found that 92 percent were interested in a two-year degree in labor studies.[40] Partly in response to this demand, the department urged three community colleges in Detroit and Flint to establish an associate degree in the field. In 1968 the schools announced that they would follow the UAW's recommendation.

The degree also fulfilled important objectives of the union's leaders. The social-science perspective permeating the curriculum would inculcate students in the Reuther philosophy of "social unionism":

> what is required is the establishment of an associate degree in cooperation with community and junior colleges where workers, union leaders and students can acquire a greater understanding of the enlarged body of knowledge uncovered by a behavioral and social science. Only such a "liberal education" can better equip union leaders and students of the labor movement to integrate itself dynamically in the total society.[41]

The tuition-benefit plan promised the financial base from which labor studies degrees could be expanded. All that was needed was for management to be cajoled into bending the "job-related" restriction to permit this kind of training. The willingness of management to subsidize labor relations and personnel courses for their supervisory corps, even "on the clock," encouraged union educators in the UAW and other organizations to seek a more evenhanded policy. The auto industry would not finance noncredit labor education, but it found degree programs more acceptable. Through deft bargaining, the UAW set a pattern in the Chrysler negotiations of 1976 that made two-year and undergraduate programs in labor studies eligible for reimbursement.[42]

The more flexible interpretation has intensified the UAW's

campaign to establish community-college degrees. In areas where membership is concentrated, such as St. Louis, Baltimore, and Flint, the union has started programs, recruited students, found staff, and provided curriculum materials.

But will the "social union" vision of UAW educators appeal to the rank and file? It is unlikely that the Education Department's strategy of promoting associate degrees will significantly increase the low participation rate—1.5 percent—of those eligible to draw on the funds.[43] The existence of labor studies courses may be the source of a college's initial attraction to a worker. But once there, his interests may depart from the goals of the program. Other subjects and courses may look more interesting. At Dundalk Community College in Baltimore, about 200 union students drawn there by practical labor courses shifted from labor studies into other fields.[44] The best recruits for the two-year degrees are not likely to be ordinary rank and filers but union activists whose ambitions and loyalties can withstand the temptations offered by a general education.

The experience of the Weekend College at Wayne State University in Detroit demonstrates that a broader program not limited to labor studies will be popular with workers. The college, which has succeeded in getting other institutions to adopt its model, has been particularly effective in recruiting auto workers. Although it has a labor component, the curriculum is at heart one in classical, general education. Students must do a year of course work in each of three interdisciplinary areas—social science, urban humanities, and science and technology—as part of the requirements for a bachelor's in general studies.[45] Its example prompted Lois Gray, director of extension for Cornell's School of Industrial and Labor Relations, at the 1980 spring conference of the UCLEA to urge labor educators to develop a more comprehensive curriculum for workers.[46]

Even among those auto workers who stick with a labor studies major, there will be many who see the degrees as a springboard out of the union ranks. The dream of self-employment, which Ely Chinoy found animated the auto workers he interviewed, is still strong.[47] These desires are intense among the skilled tradesmen in the auto plants, a group that is likely to be disproportionately represented among the recruits to educational programs. A credential to an industrial craftsman may look like a ticket to a job as foreman or a route to a small business.

The influence of the skilled tradesmen, the group from which the UAW has drawn many of its leaders, makes it unlikely that "labor studies" will be the overriding theme in the union's training efforts. Many of these workers will want journeyman retraining courses and demand that the union run apprenticeship classes to replenish their ranks. (The UAW received a Department of Labor grant of $322,936 in 1978 to register 1,000 new apprentices under national standards.)[48] The UAW has longer standing relationships with community colleges, like Henry Ford Community College in Detroit, in the area of apprenticeship than they do in labor studies.

The International Union of Electrical Workers, another large industrial union, launched an educational experiment that also revealed the wide-ranging interests of blue-collar workers. In 1969 the union began a program, whose cornerstone was the training of local union educational counselors, to assist workers in making better use of the opportunities for training in their communities. This "educational advancement" project got additional impetus from the tuition refund of $400, negotiated with General Electric and Westinghouse and available to workers as of January 1, 1971.[49].

The project kindled interests that went far beyond the confines of labor education. To be sure, members wanted union-related courses, but they also wanted to learn skills required for job advancement, such as air-conditioning, tool design, drafting, and tabulating. Other interests emerged that are not so easily categorized—car repair, reading techniques, preretirement preparation, and consumer skills, to name a few. Workers also saw a chance to involve their whole families in the process of further learning. As a result of the program, 860 workers obtained their GEDs, and 230 entered college.[50] Paul Jennings, then president of the union, emphasized the mixture of educational goals that inspired the project:

> We want to provide the opportunity for each member to send his children to college, and the opportunity to every member to expand his understanding of his Union and his job, the opportunity to every member to learn more about the social and political life of our country. . . .
>
> We must use the public school system to help every IUE member needing one, get a high school diploma, or its equivalent. We must utilize the labor education centers attached to the labor centers around the country to improve our abilities as union leaders and stewards. We must use more government funds to expand the job training programs, to provide skill and upgrading opportunities to help IUE members. Our young members know that they will probably have to change skills five or six times during the course of their lifetimes.[51]

Notes

1. William Abbott, "College/Labor Union Cooperation," reprint, *Community and Junior College Journal* (April 1977): 1–2.

2. Ibid., p. 2.

3. *Cooperation*, Service Center for Community College–Labor Union Cooperation, April, 1977, p. 4; "The Future of Education and Work," speech by William Abbott at the Labor Educator's Symposium, Pittsburgh, May 21, 1977, p. 2.

4. *Associate Degrees for Apprentices: The Operating Engineers Dual Enrollment Program*, excerpted from the final report to the National Joint Apprenticeship and Training Committee for Operating Engineers (December 31, 1975) by A. Michael Collins, associate director, Department of Education and Training, International Union of Operating Engineers, Service Center for Community College-Labor Union Cooperation, American Association of Community and Junior Colleges, Washington, D.C., 1977, p. 3.

5. Telephone interview with A. Michael Collins (see note 4), February 16, 1978; Reporter Staff, "A Degree and a Union Card," *Technical Education Reporter* (May–June 1974), p. 78.

6. Interview with A. Michael Collins.

7. "Soon: A College Degree for Union Apprentices," 1979 Laborite, p. 2.

8. For documentation on the weakening of the membership base of private-sector unions, see Helen Dewar, "Union Members Down 767,000 Over Two Years," *The Washington Post*, September 3, 1977, p. A1.

9. Mike Causey, "U.S. Union Membership Dips," *The Washington Post*, September 5, 1977, p. C2; "Public Sector Unions Show Steady Gains," *AFL-CIO News*, March 13, 1976, p. 1.

10. Causey, "Union Membership Dips," C2; Dewar, "Union Members Down," pp. A1–A2.

11. *National League of Cities et al. v. Usery, Secretary of Labor*, June 24, 1976.

12. See Lee Dembart, "The Public Disdain of Public Employees," *New York Times*, "The News of the Week in Review," June 27, 1976, p. 3.

13. For discussions on the limitations on the scope of bargaining in the public sector, see Lee C. Shaw, "The Development of State and Federal Laws," in Sam Zagoria (ed.), *Public Workers and Public Unions* (Englewood Cliffs, N.J.: Prentice-Hall, 1972), pp. 29–31. Also useful is Derek C. Bok and John T. Dunlop, *Labor and the American Community* (New York: Simon and Schuster, 1970), pp. 326–28.

14. *Executive Order 11491 as Amended, Labor Management Relations in the Federal Service*, as Amended by Executive Orders 11616, and 11638, and 11838, reprinted in *Labor-Management Relations in the Federal Service*, United States Federal Labor Relations Council, Washington, D.C., 1975, pp. 12–13.

15. *University and College Labor Education Association, State, County, and Municipal Employees Labor Education Training Needs Survey*, John R. Mac-Kenzie, project director, project funded by U.S. Department of Labor, March 1975, makes the case for the unmet need for training among the public-sector unions.

16. William Abbott, "The New Workers Education," pamphlet, Service Center for Community College-Labor Union Cooperation, American Association of Community and Junior Colleges, August 1977, p. 2.

17. On the role of supervisors in public-sector unionism, see Sterling Spero and John M. Capozzola, *The Urban Community and Its Unionized Bureaucracies* (New York: Dunellen, 1973) pp. 145–48.

18. *Cooperation*, p. 3.

19. Herbert A. Levine, *Strategies for the Application of Foreign Legislation on Paid Education Leave to the United States Scene*, National Institute of Education, Career Education Program, U.S. Department of Health, Education, and Welfare, p. 61. *The Education Fund of District Council 37: A Case Study* (Washington, D.C.: National Manpower Institute, 1979), pp. 30, 37.

20. Spero and Capozzola, *The Urban Community*, p. 213.

21. *Cooperation*, Service Center for Community College–Labor Union Cooperation, January 1978, p. 3.

22. *District Council 37*, p. 84.

23. Levine, *Strategies*, p. 67.

24. The study was Larry Matlack and Charles L. Wright, "Two Nontraditional Programs of Higher Education for Union Members: An Evaluation of the Labor–Liberal Arts Program, New York School of Industrial and Labor Relations and the DC37 Campus of the College of New Rochelle," report to Carnegie Corporation of New York, Industrial Research Unit, The Wharton School, University of Pennsylvania, Philadelphia, October 1975.

25. Levine, *Strategies*, pp. 65–66.

26. Interview with Herbert E. Levine, Bangor, Maine, April 7, 1977.

27. Al Nash, "Labor College and Its Student Body," *Labor Studies Journal* 1, no. 3 (Winter 1977): 255–58.

28. Ibid., p. 256.

29. These and other instances of the expansion of the scope of bargaining are discussed incisively in Spero and Capozzola, *The Urban Community*, pp. 173–95.

30. Ibid., p. 195.

31. "The Future of Education and Work," speech by William Abbott, p. 6.

32. A. H. Raskin, "Unions Have a Large Stake in Keeping the City Afloat," *New York Times*, February 27, 1977.

33. This figure was cited by Carroll Hutton, former education director of the UAW, in his speech to the University College Labor Education Association Annual Education Conference, Boulder, Colorado, April 8, 1976.

34. Ibid.

35. See Levine, *Strategies*, pp. 43–45, for information on the evolution of the UAW's bargaining on educational benefits. Leonard Woodcock, speech prepared for Third Annual Joint Labor Education Conference, Walter and May Reuther UAW Family Education Center, UAW Education Department pamphlet, 1977, p. 9. See also *UAW's Tuition Refund Program*, Publication #404, Detroit, UAW Education Department, 1974.

36. Barry E. Stern, *Toward a Federal Policy on Education and Work* (Washington, D.C.: U.S. Department of Health, Education, and Welfare, 1977), p. 94.

37. *UAW's Tuition Refund Program*, p. 13.

38. *Labor Organization Participation in National Employment and Training Programs* (Washington, D.C.: U.S. Department of Labor, Employment and Training Administration, 1977), p. 1.

39. Carroll Hutton speech at Boulder, Colorado.

40. *Objectives—Proposals, Policies and Guidelines for the Associate Degree in Labor Studies Program, the Two-Plus Two Joint Community College/University Program, The Four-Year University Baccalaureate Program with a Major in Labor Studies*, Detroit, UAW Education Department, 1974, p. 4.

41. Ibid., p. 5.

42. *Inter-Office Communication*, To: All Education Department Staff,

From: Carroll M. Hutton, Subject: Tuition Fund Increase—Credited Labor Studies Program, November 12, 1976, p. 1.

43. William Abbott in "Workers Will Go To College . . . If We Tell Them About Us," leaflet, Service Center for Community College-Labor Union Cooperation, American Association of Community and Junior Colleges, Washington D.C., n.d., cites this statistic in reference to an unnamed major industry, unmistakably the auto industry.

44. Interview with William Abbott, director, Service Center for Community College-Labor Union Cooperation, American Association of Community and Junior Colleges, March 1, 1978.

45. See P. Bertelsen, P. Fordham, and J. London, *Evaluation of the Wayne State University's University Studies and Week-end College Programme* (Paris: UNESCO, 1977).

46. Remarks of Lois Gray at panel session, "New Directions in University Educational Programs for Workers," University and College Labor Education Association Meetings, Hyatt Regency Hotel, Dearborn, Michigan, March 26, 1980.

47. Ely Chinoy, *Automobile Workers and the American Dream* (Boston: Beacon Press, 1955). Lawrence Rogin drew my attention to the bearing that Chinoy's book had on this issue in labor education.

48. *Cooperation*, Service Center for Community College–Labor Union Cooperation, January 1978, p. 2.

49. The IUE program is discussed in "Final Report IUE Education Advancement Program, 1969–1972," International Union of Electrical, Radio, and Machine Workers, AFL-CIO, June 1, 1972.

50. Ibid., pp. 11–13.

51. Ibid., p. 3.

7

Conclusion

Many veteran labor educators are stunned by the emergence of colleges and universities as the dispensers of credit in labor studies. These old hands have a deep suspicion of the corrupting effects credentials can have on labor education as they knew it. Their experiences had convinced them that rising from the ranks, the Socialist Party, a residential school, or the picket line were better preparation for labor leadership than an academic class could ever be. As if to set himself apart from the fashionable credentialism in his field, Lawrence Rogin, former education director of the Textile Workers Union and of the AFL-CIO, described himself to one of my classes as a "unionist working at education" rather than a "professional working for the labor movement."

There is considerable value in further education to assist union officials in grappling with such intricate issues as pensions, government budgets, tax reform, stagflation, and industrial planning. Yet the veterans in the field are perceptive in detecting some real risks in the credentialing boom. If unions and universities promote academic training for union jobs too uncritically, they may unwittingly create a narrow stratum of officials remote from the membership. These technocrats would be bound together by their common training and command over the specialized tools of labor relations. The classroom could produce a leadership fastidious about immersing itself in the turbulence of union life. They would view their skills not as the common property of their constituents, but as expertise to be hoarded. The impulse to professionalize is a seductive one. Already some unions have handed over to lawyers such responsibilities as the presentation of NLRB or arbitration cases, once the province of their own leadership.

George Brooks, a man of wide experience in labor education, aptly characterized the union expert:

> they are interested in keeping their clients, they therefore seek to make themselves indispensable, it is frequently to their interest to obscure rather than enlighten the processes for which they are engaged, and almost all of them perform at least some functions which could be performed (even though less skillfully) by local or national representatives of the union.[1]

The best protection against this tendency is for universities not to concentrate all their energies on grooming future leadership. Their major function should be to diffuse knowledge widely among workers. Without neglecting the teaching of practical skills, programs for present and prospective staff should emphasize broad training on the role of the union in American society. This should help counteract the technocratic style. Universities might supply the forum for debate on the future of the labor movement that is usually missing in union halls.

Most probably, it will not be the labor equivalent of MBAs who take the helm of the union of the future. Men and women who combine union experience with education acquired along the way will have the advantage in seeking union posts.[2] There have always been labor leaders who have had this unique preparation. Jack Conway, Walter Reuther's chief aide, went to the University of Chicago while working at General Motors' Buick plant in that city. Walter Davis, director of the Department of Community Services of the AFL-CIO, became a union member as a Red Cap at LaGuardia Airport in New York while working his way through Columbia University. The achievement of union office by people with similar backgrounds is likely to become more common. A rank and file not satisfied with merely a high school education for themselves will be looking for evidence of training when selecting their leadership.

Despite the risks, the rise of credit in labor education seems irresistible. Labor posts will continue to go to trade unionists who have displayed political prowess in their rise through the ranks. But labor studies programs promise to be an important training ground for new officials. Labor studies degrees represent a dramatic change for a vocation in which the routes to leadership have traditionally been informal.

Notes

1. George W. Brooks, "Reflections on the Changing Character of American Trade Unions," in Proceedings of Ninth Annual Meeting of Industrial Relations Research Association, Cleveland, Ohio, December 29, 1956, p. 42.

2. In an interview, May 22, 1980, in Washington D.C., Larry Rogin made a strong case for the future role of those in leadership who got a college education while working in unionized jobs.

Bibliography

Books

Abbott, William. *Effective Union Administration*. Honolulu: Industrial Relations Center, College of Business Administration, University of Hawaii, 1967.

———. *The American Labor Heritage*. Honolulu: Industrial Relations Center, College of Business Administration, University of Hawaii, 1967.

Allen, Russell. "Impact of Trade Union Efforts on Recurrent Education," in Selma J. Mushkin, ed., *Recurrent Education*. Washington, D.C.: National Institute of Education, U.S. Department of Health, Education, and Welfare, 1973.

American Council on Education, The University of the State of New York, Project on Noncollegiate Sponsored Instruction. *A Guide to Educational Programs in Noncollegiate Organizations*. Washington, D.C. 1976.

Aronowitz, Stanley, *False Promises*. New York: McGraw-Hill, 1973.

Auletta, Ken. *The Streets Were Paved with Gold*. New York: Vintage, 1980.

Barbash, Jack. *The Practice of Unionism*. New York: Harper and Row, 1956.

———. *Universities and Unions in Workers' Education*. New York: Harper Brothers, 1955.

Baritz, Loren. *The Servants of Power*. Middletown, Ohio: Wesleyan University Press, 1960.

Barkin Solomon. *The Decline of the Labor Movement*. Santa Barbara: Center for the Study of Democratic Institutions, 1961.

157

Bell, Daniel. *The Coming of Post-Industrial Society*. New York: Basic Books, 1973.

――――. *The End of Ideology*. New York: Free Press, 1962.

――――. *Work and Its Discontents*. New York: League for Industrial Democracy, 1970.

Bernstein, Irving. *Turbulent Years*. Boston: Houghton Mifflin, 1971.

Bok, Derek C., and John T. Dunlop. *Labor and the American Community*. New York: Simon and Schuster, 1970.

Brameld, Theodore, ed. *Workers' Education in the United States*. New York: Harper Brothers, 1941.

Brody, David. "Career Leadership and American Trade Unionism," in Frederic C. Jaher, ed., *Age of Industrialism in America*. New York: Free Press, 1968.

――――. "The Emergence of Mass-Production Unionism," in John Braeman et al., eds., *Change and Continuity in Twentieth-Century America*. Columbus: Ohio State University Press, 1964.

――――. *Workers in Industrial America*. New York: Oxford University Press, 1980.

Brooks, Thomas R. *Clint: A Biography of a Labor Intellectual*. New York: Atheneum, 1978.

Cheit, Earl F. *The Useful Arts and the Liberal Tradition*. New York: McGraw-Hill, 1975.

Chinoy, Ely. *Automobile Workers and the American Dream*. Boston: Beacon Press, 1955.

Christie, Robert. "The Carpenters: Case in Point," in David Brody, ed., *The American Labor Movement*. New York: Harper and Row, 1971.

Church, Robert L. "Economists as Experts: The Rise of an Academic Profession in the United States, 1870–1920," in Lawrence Stone, ed., *The University in Society*, vol. 2. Princeton: Princeton University Press, 1974.

Cook, Alice H., and Agnes M. Douty. *Labor Education Outside the Unions*. Ithaca: New York State School of Industrial and Labor Relations, Cornell University, 1958.

Cormier, Frank, and William J. Eaton. *Reuther*. Englewood Cliffs, N.J.: Prentice-Hall, 1970.

Cremin, Lawrence. *The Transformation of the School*. New York: Vintage, 1961.

Curti, Merle. *The Growth of American Thought*. New York: Harper Brothers, 1943.

Derber, Milton. *The American Idea of Industrial Democracy*. Urbana: University of Illinois Press, 1970.

――――. *Research in Labor Problems in the United States*. New York: Random House, 1967.

Doeringer, Peter B., and Michael J. Piore. *Internal Labor Markets and Manpower Analysis.* Lexington, Mass.: D. C. Heath and Co., 1971.

Dunham, E. Alden. *Colleges of the Forgotten Americans.* New York: McGraw-Hill, 1969.

Dunlop, John T., and Neal W. Chamberlain, eds. *Frontiers of Collective Bargaining.* New York: Harper & Row, 1967.

————. *Industrial Relations Systems.* New York: Henry Holt and Company, 1958.

Dwyer, Richard E. *Labor Education in the United States: An Annotated Bibliography.* Metuchen, N.J.: Scarecrow Press, 1977.

Eby, Kermit. *Protests of an Ex-organization Man.* Boston: Beacon Press, 1961.

Eddy, Edward Danforth, Jr., *Colleges for Our Land and Time.* New York: Harper Brothers, 1957.

Edwards, Harry T. "The Impact of Private Sector Principles in the Public Sector: Bargaining Rights for Supervisors and the Duty to Bargain," in David B. Lipsky, ed., *Union Power and Public Policy.* Ithaca: New York State School of Industrial and Labor Relations, Cornell University, 1975.

Etzioni, Amitai, ed. *The Semi-Professions and Their Organizations.* New York: Free Press, 1967.

Fleming, R. W. *The Labor Arbitration Process.* Urbana: University of Illinois Press, 1965.

Fogel, Walter, and Archie Kleingartner, eds. *Contemporary Labor Issues.* Belmont, Calif.: Wadsworth Publishing Company, 1966.

Golden, Clinton, and Harold J. Ruttenberg. *The Dynamics of Industrial Democracy.* New York: Harper Brothers, 1942.

Goldman, Frieda H., ed. *Reorientation in Labor Education.* Chicago: The Center for the Study of Liberal Education for Adults, 1962.

Goulden, Joseph C. *Meany.* New York: Atheneum, 1972.

Greenstone, J. David. *Labor in American Politics.* New York: Vintage, 1969.

Grob, Gerald. *Workers and Utopia.* Evanston: Northwestern University Press, 1961.

Gutman, Herbert G. *Work, Culture, and Society in Industrializing America.* New York: Alfred A. Knopf, 1976.

Hardman, J. B. S., and Maurice F. Neufeld, eds. *The House of Labor.* New York: Prentice-Hall, 1951.

Harrington, Fred Harvey. *The Future of Adult Education.* San Francisco: Jossey-Bass, 1977.

Harrington, Michael. *The Retail Clerks.* New York: John Wiley & Sons, 1962.

Hentoff, Nat, ed. *The Essays of A. J. Muste*. Indianapolis: Bobbs-Merrill, 1967.

Hicks, Clarence J. *My Life in Industrial Relations*. New York: Harper Brothers, 1941.

Hodgen, Margaret T. *Workers Education in England and the United States*. London: Kegan, Paul, Trench, Trubner, and Co., 1925.

Hofstadter, Richard. *Anti-Intellectualism in American Life*. New York: Vintage, 1963.

————, and C. Dewitt Hardy. *The Development and Scope of Higher Education in the United States*. New York: Columbia University Press, 1952.

Howe, Irving, and B. J. Widlick. *The UAW and Walter Reuther*. New York: Random House, 1949.

Hughes, Everett C. "Higher Education and the Professions," in Carl Kaysen, ed., *Content and Context*. New York: McGraw-Hill, 1973.

Hunnius, Gerry; G. David Garson; and John Case, eds. *Workers' Control*. New York: Vintage, 1973.

International Labor Office. *The Role of Universities in Workers Education*. Geneva, 1974.

Jencks, Christopher, and David Riesman. *The Academic Revolution*. Garden City, N.Y.: Anchor Books, 1969.

Jenkins, David. *Job Power*. New York: Penguin Books, 1974.

Johnson, Haynes, and Nick Kotz. *The Unions*. New York: Pocket Books, 1972.

Josephson, Matthew. *Sidney Hillman: Statesman of American Labor*. Garden City, N.Y.: Doubleday, 1952.

Karson, Marc. *American Labor Unions and Politics, 1900–1918*. Carbondale: Southern Illinois University Press, 1958.

Kerrison, Irvine L. H. *Workers' Education at the University Level*. New Brunswick: Rutgers University Press, 1957.

Larson, Magali Sarfatti. *The Rise of Professionalism*. Berkeley: University of California Press, 1977.

Laslett, John H. M., and Seymour Martin Lipset, eds. *Failure of a Dream*. Garden City, N.Y.: Anchor Press/Doubleday, 1974.

————. *Labor and the Left*. New York: Basic Books, 1970.

Lens, Sidney. *The Crisis of American Labor*. New York: A. S. Barnes, 1959.

Lester, Richard A. *As Unions Mature*. Princeton: Princeton University Press, 1958.

Levine, Herbert A. "Labor-Management Policies on Educational Opportunities," in Selma J. Mushkin, ed., *Recurrent Education*. Washington, D.C.: National Institute of Education, U.S. Department of Health, Education, and Welfare, 1973.

————. "Union-University and Inter-University Cooperation in Workers'

Education in the United States," in International Labor Office, *The Role of Universities in Workers Education*. Geneva, 1974.

Levinson, Andrew. *The Working-Class Majority*. New York: Coward, McCann, and Geoghegan, 1974.

Lipset, Seymour. *First New Nation*. New York: Basic Books, 1963.

———. *Political Man*. New York: Anchor Books, 1960.

———, and Reinhard Bendix. *Social Mobility in Industrial Society*. Berkeley and Los Angeles: University of California Press, 1976.

Lubell, Samuel. *The Future of American Politics*. New York: Harper & Row, Colophon Books, 1965.

McConnell, Grant. *The Decline of Agrarian Democracy*. New York: Atheneum, 1969.

———. *Private Power and American Democracy*. New York: Vintage, 1970.

MacLeech, Bert. "Workers' Education in the United States." Ph.D. dissertation, Harvard University Graduate School of Education. 1951.

Marquart, Frank. *An Auto Worker's Journal*. University Park: Penn State University Press, 1955.

Metzger, Walter P. *Academic Freedom in the Age of the University*. New York: Columbia University Press, 1955.

Michels, Robert. *Political Parties*. New York: Crowell-Collier, 1962.

Miernyk, William H. *Trade Unions in the Age of Affluence*. New York: Random House, 1962.

Mills, C. Wright. *New Men of Power: America's Labor Leaders*. New York: Harcourt, Brace and Co., 1948.

Mire, Joseph. *Labor Education*. Inter-University Labor Education Committee, 1956.

Montgomery, David. *Workers' Control in America*. New York: Cambridge University Press, 1979.

Morris, James O. *Conflict Within the AFL: A Study of Craft Versus Industrial Unionism, 1901–1938*. Ithaca: Cornell University Press, 1958.

Nash, Al, and May Nash. *Labor Unions and Labor Education*. Monograph Series, no. 1. University Labor Education Association, 1970.

O'Connor, James. *The Fiscal Crisis of the State*. New York: St. Martin's Press, 1973.

Ozanne, Robert. "The Wisconsin Idea in Workers' Education," in *School for Workers 35th Anniversary Papers*. Madison, Wisconsin: The School For Workers, The University of Wisconsin, 1960.

Peck, Sidney M. *The Rank-and-File Leader*. New Haven: College and University Press, 1963.

Pelling, Henry. *American Labor*. Chicago: University of Chicago Press, 1960.

Perlman, Selig. *A Theory of the Labor Movement*. New York: Macmillan, 1928.

Pierson, Frank C., et al. *The Education of American Businessmen*. New York: McGraw-Hill, 1959.

Riesman, David; Joseph Gusfield; and Zelda Gamson. *Academic Values and Mass Education*. Garden City, N.Y.: Anchor Books, 1971.

————. *Constraint and Variety in American Education*. Garden City, N.Y. Anchor Books, 1958.

Rogin, Lawrence. "How Far Have We Come in Labor Education?" in *The Labor Movement: A Re-examination*. Madison: University of Wisconsin Industrial Relations Research Institute, 1967.

————, and Marjorie Rachlin. *Labor Education in the United States*. Washington, D.C.: National Institute of Labor Education, 1968.

Ross, Dorothy. "The Development of the Social Sciences," in Alexandra Oleson and John Voss, eds., *The Organization of Knowledge in Modern America*. Baltimore: Johns Hopkins University Press, 1979.

Sayles, Leonard, and George Strauss. *The Local Union: Its Place in the Industrial Plant*. New York: Harcourt, Bruce and World, 1967.

Schwartztrauber, Ernest E. *Workers Education: A Wisconsin Experiment*. Madison: University of Wisconsin Press, 1942.

Sennett, Richard, and Jonathan Cobb. *The Hidden Injuries of Class*. New York: Vintage, 1972.

Sheed, Wilfred. *Three Mobs*. New York: Sheed and Ward, 1974.

Sheppard, Harold C., and Neal Q. Herrick. *Where Have All the Robots Gone?* New York: Free Press, 1972.

Spero, Sterling D. *Government as Employer*. New York: Remsen Press, 1948.

————, and John M. Capozzola. *The Urban Community and Its Unionized Bureaucracies*. New York: Dunellen, 1973.

Stanley, David T. *Managing Local Government Under Pressure*. Washington, D.C.: Brookings Institution, 1972.

Stern, Barry E. *Toward a Federal Policy on Education and Work*. Washington, D.C.: U.S. Department of Health, Education, and Welfare, 1977.

Stieber, Jack. *Governing the UAW*. New York: John Wiley & Sons, 1962.

————. *Public Employee Unionism: Structure, Growth, Policy*. Washington, D.C.: Brookings Institution, 1973.

Swados, Harvey. *A Radical's America*. Boston: Little, Brown & Co., 1962.

Tannenbaum, Frank. *A Philosophy of Labor*. New York: Alfred A. Knopf, 1951.

The School for Workers, The University of Wisconsin. *School for Workers 35th Anniversary Papers*. Madison, 1960.

Thernstrom, Stephan. *The Other Bostonians*. Cambridge: Harvard University Press, 1973.

Ulman, Lloyd, ed. *Challenges to Collective Bargaining*. Englewood Cliffs, N.J.: Prentice-Hall, 1967.

————. *The Government of the Steel Workers' Union*. New York: John Wiley & Sons, 1962.

————. *The Rise of the National Trade Union*. Cambridge: Harvard University Press, 1955.

Van Tine, Warren R. *The Making of the Labor Bureaucrat*. Amherst: University of Massachusetts Press, 1973.

Veysey, Lawrence R. *The Emergence of the American University*. Chicago: University of Chicago Press, 1965.

Ware, Caroline. *Labor Education in Universities*. New York: American Labor Education Service, 1946.

Wellington, Harry H., and Ralph K. Winter. *The Unions and the Cities*. Washington, D.C.: Brookings Institution, 1971.

Welter, Rush. *Popular Education and Democratic Thought in America*. New York: Columbia University Press, 1962.

Widick, B J. *Labor Today*. Boston: Houghton Mifflin, 1964.

Wiebe, Robert H. *The Search for Order*. New York: Hill & Wang, 1967.

Wilensky, Harold L. *Intellectuals in Labor Unions*. Glencoe, Ill.: Free Press, 1956.

————. *Organizational Intelligence*. New York: Basic Books, 1967.

Zagoria, Sam, ed. *Public Workers and Public Unions*. Englewood Cliffs, N.J.: Prentice-Hall, 1972.

Articles

Abbott, William. "College/Labor Union Cooperation." Reprint. *Community and Junior College Journal*, April 1977.

————. "Work in the Year 200." *The Futurist* 11 (February 1977).

Adams, James Ring, and Daniel Hertzberg. "New York's Ranking Power Broker." *Wall Street Journal*, March 7, 1979.

Allen, Russell. "The Professional in Unions and his Educational Preparation." *Industrial and Labor Relations Review* 16, no. 1 (October 1962).

Brody, David. "The Old Labor History and the New: In Search of an American Working Class." *Labor History* 20, no. 1 (Winter 1979).

Camp, Charles B. "UAW's Doug Fraser is Due to Lead Union in an Era of Changes." *Wall Street Journal*, January 26, 1977.

Causey, Mike. "U.S. Union Membership Dips." *The Washington Post*, September 5, 1977.

Cooperation. Service Center for Community College-Labor Union Cooperation, American Association of Community and Junior Colleges, April 1977.

————. January 1978.

Day, Edmund Ezra. "The School at Cornell University." *Industrial and Labor Relations Review* 3, no. 2 (January 1950).

Dembert, Lee. "Jack Bigel Holds Many Keys to City's Mansions. *New York Times*, December 11, 1976.

————. "The Public Disdain of Pulbic Employees." *New York Times*, "The News of the Week in Review," June 27, 1976.

Derber, Milton. "Divergent Tendencies in Industrial Relations Research." *Industrial and Labor Relations Review* 17, no. 4 (July 1964).

Dewar, Helen. "Union Members Down 767,000 Over Two Years." *The Washington Post*, September 3, 1977.

Dwyer, Richard E.; Miles E. Galvin; and Simeon Larson. "Labor Studies: In Quest of Industrial Justice." *Labor Studies Journal* 2, no. 2 (Fall 1977).

"Eggheads who help run unions." *Business Week*, November 11, 1961.

Eiger, Norman. "Labor Education: A Past and Future View." *The New Jersey Adult Educator* Winter 1975.

————. "Toward a National Commitment to Workers' Education: The Rise and Fall of the Campaign to Establish a Labor Extension Service, 1942–1950." *Labor Studies Journal* 1, no. 2 (Fall 1976).

Filippelli, Ronald. "The Uses of History in the Education of Workers." *Labor Studies Journal* 5, no. 1 (Spring 1980).

Geltman, Emanuel, and Irving Howe. "The Tradition of Reutherism." An Interview with Brendan Sexton. *Dissent* Winter 1972.

Glazer, Nathan. "The Schools of the Minor Professions." *Minerva* 12, no. 3 (July 1974).

Golatz, Helmut J. "Labor Studies: New Kid on Campus." *Labor Studies Journal* 2, no. 1 (Spring 1977).

Gordon, Suzanne. "Washington's Instant University." *Change* February 1976.

Gornick, Vivian. "Jack Bigel a Marxist Among the Millionaries." *Village Voice*, November 8, 1976.

Gray, Lois S. "Academic Degrees for Labor Studies: A New Goal for Unions." *Monthly Labor Review* 100, no. 6 (June 1977).

————. "The American Way in Labor Education." *Industrial Relations* 5, no. 2 (February 1966).

————. "Labor Studies Credit and Degree Programs: A Growth Sector of Higher Education." *Labor Studies Journal* 1, no. 1 (May 1976).

————. "Trends in Selection and Training of International Union Staff: Implications for University and College Labor Education." *Labor Studies Journal* 5, no. 1 (Spring 1980).

Jacobson, Robert L. "Unions Foresee Thousands of Members Enrolling in College Courses." *The Chronicle of Higher Education* 14, no. 13 (May 16, 1977).

The Journal of Educational Sociology 20, no. 8 (April 1947). (The theme of this issue is the role of industrial relations in American education.)

Levine, Herbert. "Union-University Co-operation in Labour Education." *Labour Education*, no. 30 (April 1976).

————. "Will Labour Educators Meet Today's Challenges?" *Industrial Relations* 5, no. 2 (February 1966).

Lieberthal, Mil. "On the Academization of Labor Education." *Labor Studies Journal* 1, no. 3 (Winter 1977).

Lynd, Staughton, and Al Nash. "What's Wrong with Workers Education—and What's Right." *American Teacher*, December 1972.

MacKenzie, John. "The Role of the University and College Labor Education Association in Promoting the Orderly Expansion of University Labor Education." *Labor Studies Journal* 1, no. 1 (May 1976).

Magnuson, Robert. "Lessons in Socialism at a School for Labor Leaders." *New York Times*, April 12, 1979.

Marx, Leo. "Thoughts on the Origin and Character of the American Studies Movement." *American Quarterly* 31, no. 3 (Bibliography Issue, 1979).

Nash, Al. "The University Labor Educator: A Marginal Occupation." *Industrial and Labor Relations Review* 32, no. 1 (October 1978).

Piore, Michael J. "Fragments of a 'Sociological' Theory of Wages." *The American Economic Review* 63, no. 2 (May 1973).

"Public Sector Unions Show Steady Gains." *AFL-CIO News*, March 13, 1976.

Raskin, A. H. "Lane Kirkland: New Style for Labor." *New York Times Magazine*, October 28, 1979.

————. "Unions Have a Large Stake in Keeping the City Afloat." *The New York Times*, February 27, 1977.

————. "Unions Turning to the Law and College for Top Officials." *The New York Times*, June 22, 1977.

Reporter Staff. "A Degree and a Union Card." *Technical Education Reporter* May-June 1974.

Rogin, Lawrence. "Survey of Workers Education." *Journal of the American Labor Education Service*, 30th Anniversary Issue, 1958.

Serrin, William. "Labor Facing Major Challenges as It Plans for Leadership Shift," *New York Times*, November 15, 1979.

————. "Shanker Juggles Politics and Contracts." *New York Times*, July 11, 1980.

Singer, James W. "Labor Lobbyists Go on the Defensive As Political Environment Turns Hostile." *National Journal* 12, no. 11 (March 15, 1980).

"Socialism is no longer a dirty word to labor." *Business Week*, September 24, 1979.

"Soon: A College Degree for Union Apprentices." *The 1979 Laborite*, 1979.

Starr, Mark. "The Search for New Incentives." *Industrial and Labor Relations Review* 3, no. 2 (January 1950).

———. "Unions Look at Education in Industrial Relations." *The Journal of Educational Sociology* 20, no. 8 (April 1947).

Stetson, Damon. "Union Members Broaden Their Vistas at Labor College Here." *New York Times*, September 4, 1972.

Strauss, George, and Peter Feuille. "Industrial Relations Research: A Critical Analysis." *Industrial Relations* 17, no. 3 (October 1978).

"The School: Education in the Crossroads." *Industrial and Labor Relations Report* 13, no. 1 (Fall 1976).

Tyler, Gus. "The University and the Labor Union." *Change Magazine* 2, no. 1 (February 1979).

Ulriksson, Vidkun. "The Scope, Functions, and Limitations of University Workers Education Programs." *Industrial and Labor Relations Review* 5, no. 2 (January 1952).

Weaver, Warren, Jr. "A Pinpoint System Is Developed for Finding Voters for an Issue." *New York Times*, February 3, 1979.

Wise, Gene. " 'Paradigm Dramas' in American Studies: A Cultural and Institutional History of the Movement." *American Quarterly* 31, no. 3 (Bibliography Issue, 1979).

"Young-Turk Network: New Force in Unions." *U.S. News and World Report*, March 19, 1979.

Reports, Speeches, Memoranda, and Other Documents

American Association of Community and Junior Colleges. *Organized Labor and Community Colleges*. Report of the AACJC-UAW-AFL-CIO Assembly, Washington, D.C., December 8–10, 1975. Washington, D.C., 1976.

AFL-CIO Education Department. *Conference Report of the 1972 Annual AFL-CIO Labor Education Conference*. Washington, D.C., 1973.

———. *Proposal for a National Labor Studies Center*. Washington, D.C., 1969.

———. *University Labor Education Advisory Committees*. Washington, D.C., 1976.

———. *Summary of Proceedings 1976 Annual AFL-CIO Education Conference on Labor Education, Economics Education, and Women in the Labor Movement*. Washington, D.C., 1976.

Abbott, William. "The Future of Education and Work." Speech, Labor Educator's Symposium, Pittsburgh, Pennsylvania, May 21, 1977.

———. "The New Workers Education." Pamphlet. Washington, D.C.: Service Center for Community College-Labor Union Cooperation, American Association of Community and Junior Colleges, 1977.

——— "Workers Will Go to College . . . If We Tell Them About Us." Leaflet. Washington, D.C.: Service Center for Community College-Labor Union Cooperation, American Association of Community and Junior Colleges, n.d.

Bertelsen, P.; P. Fordham; and John London. *Evaluation of the Wayne State University's University Studies and Week-end College Programme.* Paris: UNESCO, 1977.

Boyle, George V. *Report of the President.* UCLEA Annual Meeting, Boulder, Colorado, April 9, 1976.

Brooks, George W. "Reflections on the Changing Character of American Trade Unions," in *Proceedings of Ninth Annual Meeting of Industrial Relations Research Association,* Cleveland, Ohio, December 28, 29, 1956.

———. "The Relevance of Labor History to Industrial Relations," in *Proceedings of Fourteenth Annual Meeting of Industrial Relations Research Association,* New York, December 28–29, 1961.

Collins, A. Michael. *Associate Degrees for Apprentices: The Operating Engineers Dual Enrollment Program.* Washington, D.C.: Service Center for Community College-Labor Union Cooperation, American Association of Community and Junior Colleges, 1977.

Comments on the Proposal for a Master of Arts Degree in Labor Studies, n.d.

Comments on the Summary Report and Recommendations and Other Reports of the Education Committee for Rutgers University IMLR and Graduate and Undergraduate Degree Programs for Industrial Relations and Labor Studies, n.d.

Cornell New York School of Industrial and Labor Relations, Metropolitan District. *The ILR School's Labor Studies Certificate Program.* New York, 1972.

Department of Labor Studies, Penn State University. *Annual Report of Activities September 1, 1975–August 31, 1976.*

Education Amendments S. 2657.

Effective Cooperation Between Universities and Unions in Labor Education, reprinted in Lawrence Rogin and Marjorie Rachlin, *Labor Education in the United States.* Washington, D.C.: National Institute of Labor Education, 1969.

FPM Letter No. 250–3; Subject: Labor-Management Skills for New Personnel Officers. September 20, 1973.

Federal City College School of Business and Public Management. *Catalog 1975–6.* Washington, D.C., 1975.

George Meany Center for Labor Studies. *Report to Board of Trustees.* Silver Spring, Maryland, 1977.

School of Graduate Studies, Federal City College. *Guidelines for Development and Approval of Graduate Degree Programs at Federal City College,* 1976.

Gray, Lois S. *Rutgers University Master of Education with a Concentration in Labor Studies,* n.d.

International Union of Electrical, Radio, and Machine Workers, AFL-CIO. *Final Report IUE Educational Advancement Program, 1969–1972.* Washington, D.C., 1972.

Inter-Office Communication, To: All Education Department Staff, From: Carroll M. Hutton, Subject: Tuition Fund Increase, Credited Labor Studies Program. Detroit, November 12, 1976.

Joint Statement on Effective Cooperation Between Organized Labor and Higher Education, reprinted in *Labor Studies Journal* 1, no. 3 (Winter 1977).

Kane, Arthur. Address to Society of Federal Labor Relations Professionals, Washington, D.C., February 25, 1977.

Labor Education Center, Rutgers University. "Proposed Program for Graduate Study Leading to the Master of Arts in Labor Studies." Submitted to the Graduate School, October 1973.

Labor Relations and Research Center, University of Massachusetts, Amherst. *Annual Report Fiscal Year Ending June 30, 1976.*

————. *Roster of Graduates.*

Labor Studies Center, Division of Community Education, Federal City College. Annual Report 1971. Washington, D.C., 1971.

Labor Studies Center, School of Education, Federal City College. *Annual Report July 1, 1975 to June 30, 1976.*

————. *Equivalency Criteria for Employment and Promotion of Faculty Members in Lieu of Academic Degree and Teaching Experience.* Washington, D.C., 1977.

————. *Proposal for a Master of Arts Degree in Labor Studies.* Washington, D.C., 1976 (revised 1977).

Levine, Herbert A. "Paid Educational Leaves: Implications for Work and Education in America," in *Conference Proceedings, Designing Diversity '75,* Second National Conference on Open Learning and Nontraditional Study, Washington, D.C., June 17–19, 1975.

————. *Strategies for the Application of Foreign Legislation on Paid Educational Leave to the United States Scene.* Washington, D.C.: Career Education Program, National Institute of Education, U.S. Department of Health, Education, and Welfare.

MacKenzie, John R. "Essay on the Supply of Lifelong Learning of Workers." Invitational paper, Office of Education Lifelong Learning Project. Submitted December 22, 1978.

————. Draft chap., "Labor Education in the United States." 1977.

Matlack, Larry, and Charles L. Wright. *Two Nontraditional Programs of Higher Education for Union Members: An Evaluation of the Labor-Liberal Arts Program, New York School of Industrial and Labor Relations and the DC37 Campus of the College of New Rochelle.* Philadelphia, Pennsylvania: Industrial Research Unit, The Wharton School, University of Pennsylvania, 1975.

Memorandum. To: Dr. John M. Jenkins, Dean, School of Education, From: John R. MacKenzie, Associate Professor and Director. Subject: Program Projections for Year 1980 of the Labor Studies Center. February 17, 1976.

Memorandum. To: Dr. John Jenkins, Dean, School of Education, From: Dr. Thomas John, Chairman School of Education Curriculum Committee. Subject: Review of Labor Studies and Special Education Masters Degree Program. June 16, 1976.

Memorandum. To: Dr. Thomas John, Chairman School of Education Curriculum Committee, From: John R. MacKenzie, Associate Professor and Director. Subject: Questions Raised About Master of Arts in Labor Studies Proposal. July 2, 1976.

Memorandum. To: George Zachariah, Member Educational Policy Committee, Faculty Senate, Federal City College, From: John R. MacKenzie, Associate Professor and Director. Subject: Proposal for a Master (sic) Arts Degree Labor Studies. February 14, 1977.

Memorandum. To: Jack MacKenzie, From: Edgar Lee, on "Listing of Course Activity." February 28, 1977.

Memorandum. To: Dr. Wendell P. Russell, President, Mount Vernon Campus, University of the District of Columbia, Dr. Cleveland Dennard, President, Van Ness Campus, UDC, From: John R. MacKenzie, Associate Professor and Director. Subject: Location of the Labor Studies Center Within the Organizational Structure of the University of the District of Columbia. May 10, 1977.

Miller, John. *UCLEA Curriculum Survey*, prepared for UCLEA-Academic Policy and Degree Programs Committee, 1976.

Miller, Richard V., and David B. Lipsky. *Rutgers University Master of Arts in Industrial Relations Degree*, n.d.

Mills, C. Wright. "The Contribution of Sociology to Studies of Industrial Relations," in Proceedings of First Annual Meeting of Industrial Relations Research Association, Cleveland, Ohio, December 29–30, 1948.

Minutes, Graduate Academic Policy Committee, Federal City College, for meeting September 2, 1976.

National League of Cities et al. v. Usery, Secretary of Labor. June 24, 1976.

National Manpower Institute. *The Education Fund of District Council 37: A Case Study.* Washington, D.C., 1979.

Peters, Ronald. "Roots of Governmental Support of Labor Education, 1900–1949." Presentation, Annual Meeting of UCLEA, Ohio State University, Columbus, Ohio, April 3, 1975.

Strauss, George. "Directions in Industrial Relations Research," in Proceedings of 1978 Annual Spring Meeting of Industrial Relations Research Association, Los Angeles, California, May 11–13, 1978.

Study Committee on the Labor Relations and Research Center *Report.* Submitted, June 9, 1971.

Tinning, Paul P. *Report to the Eighth Legislature Session of 1976 on Senate Resolution 257 and Senate Concurrent Resolution 148 Relating to Labor Studies and Activities in Higher Education.* Honolulu: Center for Labor-Management Education, University of Hawaii, 1975.

Turner, J.C. "Labor and Continuing Education." Speech, Invitational Conference on Continuing Education, Manpower Policy and Lifelong Learning, January 10, 1977.

UAW Education Department. *Course Descriptions and Outlines Suggested for an Associate Degree in Labor Studies Program at the 2-Year College Level.* Detroit, 1975.

———. *Objective: Proposals, Policies, and Guidelines.* Detroit, 1974.

———. *UAW's Tuition Refund Program,* Publication #404, Detroit, UAW Education Department, 1974.

———. *Workers "Opportunity" College.* Detroit, n.d.

U.S. Department of Labor, Employment and Training Administration. *Labor Organization Participation in National Employment and Training Programs.* Washington, D.C., 1977.

United States Federal Labor Relations Council. *Executive Order 11491 as Amended, Labor Management Relations in the Federal Service, as Amended by Executive Orders 11616, and 11638, and 11838.*

University and College Labor Education Association. *State, County, and Municipal Training Needs Survey.* Washington, D.C., 1975.

Visitation Committee Report M.S. in Labor Studies. November 1976.

Whyte, William F., and Lois S. Gray. *Undergraduate Degrees in Labor Studies: Livingston College and University College.* n.d.

Winpisinger, William. "Job Satisfaction: A Trade Union Point of View." Speech, University and College Labor Education Association meeting, Black Lake, Michigan, April 15, 1973.

Witte, Edwin E. "Where We Are in Industrial Relations," in Proceedings of First Annual Meeting of Industrial Relations Research Association, Cleveland, Ohio, December 29–30, 1978.

Woodcock, Leonard. Statement prepared for the Third Annual Joint Labor Education Conference, Walter and May Reuther UAW Family Education Center, November 14, 1976. Detroit: UAW Education Department, 1977.

Yoder, Dale. "Changing University Industrial Relations Programs: On-Campus Teaching," in Proceedings of Fifteenth Annual Meeting of Industrial Relations Research Association, Pittsburgh, Pennsylvania, December 27–28, 1962.

Index

UNIONS AND UNIVERSITIES
The Rise of the New Labor Leader

by JOEL S. DENKER
with an introduction by A. H. Raskin

Labor studies programs are booming in the colleges and universities, on both undergraduate and graduate levels. Despite a continuing distrust of intellectuals, trade unions are going outside their own ranks to hire university-trained staff, and union members—present and prospective officials—are taking classes in such areas as labor history, labor and politics, collective bargaining, and labor law.

This is the first book to study the emergence of the field of labor studies, its struggle for acceptance in the academy, and its effects within the labor movement. Of particular interest is the examination of the impact of the credentials issue on the character of the American union, which has traditionally prized experience rather than education as the best preparation for labor leadership. Also discussed are the power shifts that inevitably result from the involvement of the labor movement with universities. Drawing on his own experience, particularly in developing a master's in labor studies program at the University of the District of Columbia, the author has provided anecdotal material documenting the struggle toward resolution of complex educational issues.

The book will be of particular interest to union and university labor educators, trade union officials, and government officials concerned with labor policy or workers education, as well as to academics and students in such fields as labor history, industrial relations, manpower economics, sociology, and education.

Joel Denker, who received his doctorate from the Harvard University Graduate School of Education, is associate professor of labor studies at the University of the District of Columbia. He has also taught in labor programs at Rutgers University and the State University of New York College at Old Westbury. He is co-author of No Particular Place To Go *an account of the alternative high school that he directed in Washington, D.C.*